10-21-93

To: Young

from: Troy & Evelyn
          Reed

Enjoy your visit
to Tulsa, Ok.

THE
INTERGLOBAL
REVOLUTION

THE INTERGLOBAL REVOLUTION

H.B. Chee

INTERGLOBAL, INC.
Tulsa, Oklahoma

To Cathy,
who keeps pace with
me to the beat
of a "different drummer."

Contents

PREFACE

The cover of the first issue of *Fortune* magazine in the 1990s decade told the good news, "The global march of freedom is creating vast opportunities. Seizing them will require new ways of doing business." I call this march the Interglobal Revolution. The vast array of opportunities is nothing less than the Interglobal Age.

This book chronicles the Interglobal Revolution: the fastest-ever major change in geopolitics without the use of armed forces! More importantly, the book provides strategies and tactics for capitalizing on the abundant business opportunities.

But this is most important: in devoting ourselves to world economic development, we spread freedom and we reestablish American leadership in the affairs of this planet.

PART ONE

Prologue

Chapter One

INTRODUCTION

As the June 4, 1989 sun rose at the International Dateline in the Central Pacific, a billion Chinese were still sleeping peacefully. But the quiet of Tiananmen Square in Beijing was rudely broken as elements of the People's Liberation Army began burning the vehicles barricading entry to that hundred-acre oasis of freedom. Ten thousand troops stormed the tranquil demonstrators! By sunrise, the hopes of the Chinese student freedom activists were crushed.

Four hours later, dawn signaled the timing for the first prayer of the day in Iran. Although the day's prayers were unusually fervent, Allah did not respond. Musavi Khomeini died.

The people of Poland greeted this same sun with eager expectation; throughout the long day they cast their ballots for Solidarity in the first-ever free election in a communist land. By the time the sun was high over America's amber waves of grain, Warsaw's overlords knew they had suffered a stunning defeat. The Poles had voted for freedom!

When before had a Sunday sun witnessed such historic events? December 7, 1941? Never?

THE REVOLUTION BEGINS

Most citizens of this shrinking globe stopped their weekend pursuits long enough to be emotionally drawn into a quest for freedom. They had watched, listened, and discussed their feelings. The Olympics had brought us together to play; but instant communications that day bonded billions with the souls of those in China and Poland who were standing up for freedom.

June 4th was important to the leaders of the world's nations — the powerful and the weak. It gave President Bush a Polish pulpit, in July, from which he could preach freedom to a watching world. But Hashemi Ratsanjani, speaker of the Iranian Parliament, reacted faster; it was still June when he preached

Iranian-Soviet friendship at the largest mosque in Baku, the capital of Azerbaijan Soviet Socialist Republic. Both events were without modern precedent.

Yet, historians will probably write that the greatest event of the day took place in the hearts of the masses. The message was clear: strive for freedom!

Authoritarian leaders everywhere were in for a long, hot summer. In fact, before the summer was half over, a hundred thousand Soviet coal miners, many of them Russian and almost all Slavic, were throttling their economy. Both the greatest military power and the greatest economic power on the globe had already felt the impact of June 4th in a way that would significantly alter their future — perhaps the destiny of one or both.

The ripple effect from these catalytic events has become a planetary tidal wave. America faces its finest hour. Businessmen dream of such an opportunity: owning an unlimited supply of an unrivaled product with an almost indefinite overseas market. Never have we had such an opportunity to export freedom!

Although this blood-bought freedom cost our forefathers a fearful price, America's culture has swung from sacrifice to selfishness. The "Me" generation has led the United States into moral and economic decline — certainly no position from which to export a product that has always been championed by men with the character of Patrick Henry or Mahatma Ghandi in victorious battle against oppressors.

Will Americans continue in their hedonistic pursuits and ignore the aspirations of foreign freedom fighters, and in so doing, damn our society to the fate of the Babylonian, Persian, and Roman empires? Will we, like dynasty after dynasty in China, grow, flower, become fat and then corrupt, only to finally be overwhelmed by a barbaric horde bent on plunder? What, besides a magnificent crusade to export freedom, could turn our people from their fervid, destructive consumerism and worship of the goddess of instant gratification?

OPPORTUNITY KNOCKS

For his part, President Bush emerged from the 1989 Paris Economic Summit as the unquestioned leader of the present world freedom movement. Admittedly, the United States has very limited financial resources to devote to so proud an undertaking. Our government has, therefore, adopted the role of facilitator.

We encourage the other industrialized nations to join market-oriented economic systems with Eastern Europe and with other freedom-seeking nations. More importantly, we encourage our own private sector to become involved in business ventures and in people-to-people volunteerism.

Yes, America must again lead. Bill Clinton defeated George Bush in the 1992 election because the majority of our people sent this clear signal: they care less about international affairs than they care about their own pocketbooks. But what these voters forgot is this: The business of America is business, not government. And in the business world today, the key is "Export or Perish." Although the voters forgot, President Clinton must not, and all Americans must become involved in exporting freedom, products, and technologies. Agronomist Dean McHard, who has worked in almost twenty nations, is a role model for businessmen who would join the freedom export campaign. More than twenty years ago, he elected to forego the quicker, surer profits inherent in doing business here, in order to work in the malnourished regions of the earth. He has learned to package appropriate technologies and to assist American businessmen in initiating viable enterprises that are beneficial and fair to all concerned. Often, the principles are contrary to those factors that assure success in America — they are small projects that are labor-intensive, for instance, and may even employ technologies that are obsolete in the United States. In fact, McHard reports that blindly doing everything the way it would be done "stateside" is usually imprudent, fast-food franchises and other stores merchandizing the American image being an exception.

Volunteerism is making an impact. People are impressed when Americans give their time and travel at their own expense in order to work with them. More than ten thousand Southern Baptists travel abroad each year as short-term volunteers working in vocation-related activities such as construction, farming, medicine, and dentistry. Dr. Mary Futrell, a retired Mississippi State University nutritionist, has met with hundreds of women in their huts in a dozen nations around the world, helping them provide a better diet for their families. She is an enthusiastic advocate of involvement by professional, service, and church groups. A vacation spent in service abroad tends to develop the kind of freedom-exporters America needs. Like Futrell, most find a satisfaction that they share freely with their peers. Most also change their lifestyle so that they can make annual, biannual, or triannual trips as living proof that freedom is worth whatever price must be paid for it.

We Americans now have a window of opportunity to share our well-proven system, but it will require millions of us to share a quality decision to dedicate ourselves to political action, business and professional involvement, and volunteerism; a depth of commitment to freedom that we have never made during peacetime.

But the scope of this book is restricted to business opportunities. It is focused upon timeless principles that produce profits in the fastest-changing times man has experienced.

NO REVOLUTION!

Upon his return from the storm-tossed summit conference with the Soviet president, George Bush, on December 4, 1989, described world political events as a "peaceful revolution."

December 4th. Just six action-filled months after June 4th, 1989. Revolution, indeed. Yet, it was more than a peaceful revolution. Free markets emerged. Private enterprise began to flourish in Eastern Europe. The Soviet head of state met with the Pope . . . religion openly displayed its wares in Communist countries.

The summer of the first anniversary of the Tiananmen Square massacre produced the finale to this grand wave of a unique independence movement. Communist hardliners attempted to seize the Soviet government by force, only to meet a groundswell of popular resistance. Independence soon followed for all of the republics that had been a part of the Soviet Union. They then hastily pulled themselves together into the still-nebulous Commonwealth of Independent States (C.I.S.). Popular elections were held in these now-free republics: each republic in its own way and with its own speed began creeping toward a market economy.

The changes came quickly in unexpected quarters. Even staid, conservative publishers were forced to use tabloid terms to cover the news adequately. Awesome was not an overstatement. Nor was it Madison Avenue hype. Revolutions, even peaceful ones, are awesome!

THE INTERGLOBAL REVOLUTION

What, then, shall we name this revolution? It transcended national, regional, and continental boundaries, emanating from China and moving within one Sunday to Iran and Poland. In fact, it transcended politics and government. It was also an economic revolution . . . free people wanted, and in some cases, got, free markets. Almost unbelievably, it was also a religious revolution: faith triumphed over atheistic materialism.

In the brief span of a year or so, almost everything that has been written on the subjects of geopolitics, international business, and Communism and the future of religion, was obsolete.

Indeed, what shall we name it?

Interglobal Revolution.

The day of the global village has arrived. Suddenly. With finality!

It is a revolutionary new era — in politics, in business, in spiritual realms. New principles apply. Old ones won't work — regardless of how tested and true in prerevolutionary days.

This book is written to provide timeless principles for American business in the Interglobal Age, following the Interglobal Revolution.

Chapter Two

OSMOSIS, DIFFUSION, OR EXPLOSION?

I t is trite but true: Americans do not have a proper appreciation of the freedom they enjoy. Our fullness of freedom is the exception rather than the rule in most of the world today; it is also a recent event in the chronicles of mankind.

From the beginning of recorded history, groups of humans, normally bonded by geography, ethnicity, and almost always speaking the same language, banded together for protection or for conquest under a strong leader. Freedom, human rights, and a voice in government were little known. This leader had absolute authority and was addressed by such titles as "Master" and "Lord." He sometimes even demanded worship as a god.

Deep in the heart of most people, however, there was a longing to be free; to have input into the affairs of the village. But the individual always was controlled by a person or an institution too powerful for him to challenge. In much of Asia, this person is often called "the Big Chinaman."

Not all rulers were despots. Here and there, little known to historians, citizens were granted rights. Some noble democracies actually developed . . . about three thousand years ago in India and about five hundred years later in Greece. As if by osmosis, freedom spread rapidly in both of these ancient cultures, to the great delight of the people!

THE HISTORY OF FREEDOM

Village republics in northern India had democratic governments. Affairs were managed by five elders who were elected on the basis of their wisdom and ability. Since some Aryans also migrated to Germany, Adolph Hitler claimed this common thread as a basis for his assertion that they were the "Master race."

Unfortunately for the 20th-century world, Hitler chose not to emulate Aryan democracy.

In about 500 B.C., the Greek city-states began to allow their free male citizens the right to vote in the popular assembly. Committees of the assembly served as the criminal courts.

This early democracy worked well until the practice arose of paying the elected officials. The best leaders sought these jobs and did not serve in the army. Without their direction and fighting ability in battle, democracy was extinguished for two thousand long years. The barriers to the osmosis of freedom were insuperable during this lengthy, dreary era.

OSMOSIS

Osmosis is defined as diffusion through a semipermeable membrane. In nature, substances diffuse by freely moving so that they become evenly spread within a given container or vessel, moving spontaneously from an area of higher concentration to areas of lower concentration, until a homogeneous equilibrium is reached. Plant and animal cell walls and membranes are semipermeable barriers that greatly slow the diffusion process and selectively prevent some materials from moving across the barriers.

In the geopolitical arena, the "membrane" tends to be a political boundary. During the depths of the cold war, radio broadcasts were almost the only freedom messages penetrating the Iron and Bamboo curtains. In China, it was the educational reform of Deng Xiaoping that gave the students in the late '80s access to the thoughts of Mahatma Gandhi and Martin Luther King as well as a knowledge of the freedom enjoyed by people outside their lands. It will likely be some time before the leaders in China will allow the precepts of freedom to be so easily accessed again by their young people.

BARRIERS TO FREEDOM

One of the most influential builders of barriers to freedom was a Chinese warlord named Sun Tzu. The hand of the oppressors of freedom was greatly strengthened in about the 4th century B.C. when he wrote *The Art of War*, which he sent to Ho-lu, King of Wu. The purpose of his writings was to give kings and warlords a formula for the successful prosecution of war. It is important to understand the principles laid down by Warlord Sun in order to understand why it has been so difficult to dislodge oppressive regimes and the opposition that can be expected, as America seeks to export freedom to the world.

Warlord Sun believed that military strategists should be able to subdue the enemy without engaging him; to take his cities without laying siege; to overthrow nations without great bloodshed. He understood that careful planning based on sound information of the enemy could contribute to a speedy military decision, often with an inferior military force. In his opinion, the army was simply the instrument to finally take possession of land that had previously been made vulnerable. Prior to the hostilities, secret agents separated the enemy's allies from him and conducted a variety of secret, subversive activities: infiltration, corruption, subversion of officials, the creation of internal discord and the nurturing of fifth-column movements. The spies, active at all levels in the enemy organization, provided feedback that formed the basis for the battle plan.

There are four translations of the works of Sun Tzu into the Russian language and at least one into German. It is reported that these ancient writings have greatly influenced the development of the strategies of conquest of international communism, the central feature of the 20th century.

If his writings have impacted Western military thought, how much more has his work influenced the strategies of the Chinese and the Japanese? *The Art of War* has had a profound influence throughout Chinese history. It is a source of Mao Tsetung's strategic theories and of the tactical doctrine of the People's Liberation Army of China. It was transmitted to both Japan and Russia by the conquering Mongols. Careful analysts see the Warlord Sun's influence in the Japanese operations of World War II.

Intuitively, his principles have been adopted by warlords of many races and colors up to this present moment.

The likes of Sun and his disciples continually construct membranes, even walls, which allow little opportunity for the diffusion of freedom, free markets, and free people. Niccolo Machiavelli popularized Sun's theses in the West. He promoted the belief that selfishness is somehow good, because man is self — and self must be selfish. Interestingly, he also wrote a book entitled, *The Art of War*. Could he have been a secret disciple of the warlord who lived two thousand years before his time? Probably!

DEMOCRACY MATURES

Lasting democracy emerged from Europe only a little more than a hundred years after Machiavelli penned his wicked work.

The Puritan Revolution introduced democracy to England at mid-17th century. More than a hundred years then passed before an American colonist, Thomas Jefferson, proposed that human rights, by law of nature, include life, liberty, and the ownership of property.

But the new citizens of the United States wanted guarantees. Before our Constitution was ratified by the states, freedom of religion, speech, assembly, and the press were guaranteed. Freedom had a foothold in the new world as well as the old!

The osmosis of freedom and democracy began to accelerate following the success of the American Revolution; in 1789 French citizens stormed the Bastille in Paris, and freedom came to continental Europe. Most of Latin America, under the benign eye of American presidents administering the Monroe Doctrine, shook off the shackles of Spain and Portugal in the century that followed.

Patrick Henry, on March 23, 1775, speaking in the House of Burgess in Williamsburg, Virginia Colony, ended his most famous speech like this:

> *Is life so dear, or peace so sweet, as to be purchased at*
> *the price of chains and slavery? Forbid it, almighty God!*
> *I know not what course others may take, but as for me,*
> *give me liberty or give me death!*

These wonderful words have been adopted in many lands and solemnly spoken by advocates of freedom in many languages in subsequent years. The number of persons who have, in fact, given their lives in an effort to obtain freedom for their colleagues is, without doubt, in the hundreds of millions. Other millions have languished in prison because they campaigned for freedom and human rights. Even more have, like the students in Tiananmen Square, quietly slipped away to their homes, realizing that their martyrdom at that time and place could not advance their cause. Additional billions of people have dreamed of freedom, but have lacked the courage to face death.

Unchallenged, the United States stands as the premier champion of freedom in this global village. Its Statue of Liberty is a world symbol. As good citizens of this community of nations, we must take a moderate stance, working always for freedom without "inciting a riot," as was aptly stated by Secretary of State James Baker during the student protests in Beijing.

Prudence dictates that the American government restrain itself during the course of popular uprisings: Tiananmen Square, Eastern Europe, and Azerbaijan. However, we must let the world know that we wish everyone to have the same freedoms and rights that we so often take for granted. President Bush set a good example by travelling to Poland and Hungary to quietly encourage the process of osmosis and the development of a market-oriented economy.

But not all this planet's despotic warlords are communists; some of the most ruthless are right-wing in their ideology. Some simply are only for themselves. Nevertheless, the aspiration to be free and to speak freely seeks to spread itself as naturally as the scent spreads from an aerosol container of perfume into the entire room. Warlords desperately build barriers to this diffusion. From time to time, Americans have the opportunity to take some freedom through these barriers. And freedom is such heady perfume to those who have never before inhaled it!

EXPLOSION?

Given the slow pace of the osmosis before June 4, 1989, no rational person would have projected the dramatic movement toward democracy and free markets in Eastern Europe and the former Soviet Republics in the following two years. A totally new and unexpected event took place. Mikhail Gorbachev simply removed the barriers to the diffusion of freedom and private enterprise in his European satellite nations. The pent-up pressure was so great that the movement almost proceeded with explosive rapidity in October and November! Then, just as suddenly, both Gorbachev and the Soviet Union went away.

Osmosis, diffusion, or explosion? How fast will the freedom movement spread in the future? Eastern Europe has taught us that the speed will be about as fast as the rulers allow.

American businessmen will be able to calculate business strategies based on their knowledge of the degree of freedom allowed in a given nation and the propensity of that nation for positive change.

U.S. Secretary of State James Baker III, in a December 11, 1989 speech in Berlin, declared the Interglobal Revolution to be an historic fact. The hated Wall is down. Baker said the superpowers must cooperate in developing a "new architecture for a new era."

Yes, Secretary Baker, it is a new era. The Interglobal Age.

And the American business community can help keep us a superpower in this fast-paced age — with interglobal thinking!

Chapter Three

THE TRIUMPH OF ETHICS

Sages through the ages have abhorred Warlord Sun and his kind. Unfortunately, itinerant teachers and philosophers such as Buddha, Confucius, and Jesus received little attention and had little effect upon their culture during their own lifetimes.

Confucius, born in B.C. 551, the son of a military commander of royal descent, was oriented toward the development of good government. At the age of fifteen, he set his mind on mastering the teachings of the prophet-emperors and wise men whose influence had already made China a wise and united nation.

Confucius married at the age of nineteen. By the time he was twenty-one, he had a few students, whom he taught that the secret of good government was in choosing honest and educated officials. He seemed to be on a good career pathway when he was appointed governor. His well-managed district became a wonder of his time. Soon, however, he was compelled to resign because of a jealous duke. He then travelled from place to place, trying to find a prince who would listen to his teachings of just government.

But Confucius was misunderstood and ignored by most of the rulers of his time. He died virtually unknown, after having taught for fifty years. Later, the *Five Classics*, which recorded his teachings, became textbooks. Even the emperors considered Confucius "the teacher of teachers." Central to the governmental teachings of Confucius was the just, fair, even-handed treatment of all citizens. His writings gave rise to other literary works, many of which extol the merits of morality and ethical conduct. It was a time known as the "classical" period of Chinese history — an era that abruptly came to an end when King Chao of C'hin liquidated the Chou dynasty.

Meanwhile, a great civilization had risen in the West. The Greek city-states developed a much higher form of democracy than their Asian counterparts. By the time of Pericles, about 400 B.C., every citizen of Athens had the right to appear and vote in the popular assembly and in the committees of the assembly that served as the criminal courts. This early experience with democracy was flawed in that it did not extend the rights of citizens to women and slaves. Aristotle, a leading critic, called democracy "mob rule."

A careful study of ancient history tells us this: many philosophers and holy men did not believe that common men, much less women or slaves, had the ability to wisely discern the issues and to have a meaningful say in government. Slavery was seldom challenged. On the other hand, even some rulers saw that it was in their best interest to provide justice and some human rights, but these rights did not extend to allowing opposition to their regime or to the worship of gods other than their own.

MODERN ETHICS

Thus, it remained for the Puritans in 17th-century England to further champion the ethics of justice, freedom, and human rights. The crucible of forging a civilization out of a wilderness and the flame of spiritual renewal gave rise to a frontier morality that demanded equality. It was an intellectual, Thomas Jefferson, however, who translated this emerging American ethic into words the world would understand and that would be preserved to this day.

In retrospect, the failure of almost all governments to provide basic freedoms prior to the Puritans was so that those governments could retain control. Aristotle's objection to democracy had some basis in fact — universal education has always been a keystone in the building of any enduring democracy. In 1787, when providing for the government of the Northwest Territory, the American Congress declared: "Religion, morality, and knowledge being necessary to good government and the happiness of mankind, schools and a means of education shall ever be encouraged." In the same spirit, the French Constitution of 1793 guaranteed public education.

On January 6, 1941, President Franklin D. Roosevelt said in his message to Congress that the "Four Freedoms should be the basis of the settlement to be made after World War II." These were defined as "freedom from want, freedom from fear, freedom of worship, and freedom of speech."

Faced with a number of strong isolationist congressmen who did not desire to become involved in the war against Nazi Germany, Roosevelt invoked these ethical tenets as a preamble in his request to Congress for a bill to permit the leasing of war materials to countries fighting the Axis Powers, as well as to any country whose defense was important to the United States. Later, it was popular for speakers in many nations to refer to the Four Freedoms as the ideals for which the armies allied against German, Italian, and Japanese aggression were fighting.

Today, in the enlightened '90s, no reasonable opponent can be found anywhere who will argue against the ethics of the principles of freedom expounded by Jefferson and Roosevelt. Unfortunately, warlords of any era do not debate morality: they merely seek, by whatever means are at their disposal, to impose their will and control upon as many humans as they possibly can.

"A civil society" is the term adopted by Pope John Paul II for what is being spoken of in this book as freedom. In early August, 1989, he convened a conference at his summer palace in Castel Gandolfo for the purpose of hearing what today's most distinguished philosophers and historians had to say on the subject. Participants were invited without regard to their religious convictions.

For three days, the Pope listened to everything from the fundamentals of political science to the ethics of the use of force to break the power of a totalitarian regime. Totalitarianism was defined as a government or institution that destroys all it cannot dominate. Much discussion was given to how a pluralistic society can best be organized to provide for the rights of all its citizens, yet be governable and organized. This obviously calls for constant change and constant reorganization. A common thread through the conference was the need to decentralize power yet effectively guide the community being governed, without compressing power into a critical mass in the hands of a few, which favors abuse. History has conclusively proven this: power corrupts and absolute power tends to corrupt absolutely. The notable exceptions serve only to prove this rule. So, America's founding fathers displayed great wisdom in their separation of powers into the executive, legislative, and judicial branches of government. Strong state, city, and even school-district governments are also salient strengths in the preservation of democracy.

American exporters of freedom are on solid ground. Even though we have an enduring Constitution, Bill of Rights, and two-party system, we should not seek to make other countries our clones. And, at all costs, we must never confuse our culture with freedom. We must indeed encourage the quest for freedom everywhere, while allowing latitude for creativity, culture — yes, even for trial and error. Freedom, in the sweep of the history of our race, is only now entering into its adolescence.

Nevertheless, we do well in giving political assistance, especially when, as in the sudden surge toward freedom and free markets in Eastern Europe and the former Soviet Union, nations have the grand opportunity to develop a new form of government. Be proud, Americans; we are the first to be called; we are the first to send our finest people!

Such pride, however, should not give us grounds for hasty criticism of the moral blind spots in other nations' governments. Our own system was initially an aristocratic democracy. Only male landowners who were "free, white and 21" could vote in our early agrarian system. A century passed between the war over slavery and the civil rights movement. Nevertheless, it is incumbent upon us, in a nonjudgmental way, to point out these blind spots to others in our global village. We must speed up the rate of osmosis for the benefit of all mankind.

A critical analysis of the morality of man and his leaders challenges the statement that power corrupts — perhaps it only allows the manifestation of hidden desires. In any case, checks and balances are imperative.

Karl Marx challenged the morality of the free-market economy. As the searchlight of "glasnost" revealed the true nature of the Soviet society, more inequities appeared than were found in the system Marx was so determined to exterminate. Competition tends to keep both the marketplace and government relatively honest and oriented toward the needs and wishes of the citizens. Best yet, but not perfect.

INTERGLOBAL ETHICS AND THINKING

Laziness is one of the most important reasons that American business people often do not chase overseas profit opportunities, and fail to exhibit the hustle of their East Asian competition. We are not forced to work outside of this great land, while the small island nation of Japan has no choice — it truly must export or perish. Japan imports crude oil, timber and lumber, iron ore, and a long list of raw materials, a fact that drives her to export for survival. Perhaps the British also developed their empire out of sheer necessity!

The Interglobal Revolution forces us to reexamine all of our historic assumptions. Can America continue to afford the luxury of choice when it comes to extending our enterprises outside our personal comfort zones? Outside our region? Outside North America? Do we have an ethical responsibility to the future generations of our families, to our nation, and to the sum of mankind to painfully expand our horizons? The monthly and quarterly trade data have not given us the incentive to shake off our lethargy and retool our minds. As a people, will we wait until it is too late to consider seriously that we must revise our thought process, and that this new thought process is in interglobal thinking?

In Japan, Inc., exporting is everyone's priority job. Government, labor, management, shareholders, bankers, educators, students — everyone thinks export. And, they work together with all other Japanese, even when it is not in their own short-term interest. All Americans must adopt such interglobal thinking. As Benjamin Franklin wisely stated more than two hundred years ago, "We must hang together, or we shall all hang separately." Unity was not optional then. We have reached a point in our civilization when once again it is not a viable option.

But what does this slothful self-centeredness have to do with ethics and morality? Should Benjamin Franklin be summoned to testify against us? I believe that he would show righteous indignation at the spurning of the thrift and industry that he continually taught in his writings. Franklin was not known as a religious man; how much more would our Puritan forefathers decry the deChristianization of America today? Indeed, the bulk of the citizens who have gone before would rise up and say this: "The 'Me Generation' has a grave moral problem."

There is a second, very important ethical reason why multitudes of prudent business owners and executives stay home. They do not wish to compromise their business ethics.

They have heard the horror stories that associates have shared about the lack of morality in much of the business community outside the United States and Canada. Outright theft. Womanizing. Bribery. Lies. The list is as long as it is frightening to prudent people schooled in taking only small, well-defined risks.

But the Interglobal Age is here. Are we suddenly forced to compromise our morals for the sake of our nation? Not at all! Interglobal thinking exports the moral values that made America the leader. Therefore, this book discusses the political, religious, and ethical aspects of the various types of empires with which we must deal. We will thus be able not only to export our products and technologies, but also, our ideals of freedom, human rights, and ethics.

But won't they think we are preaching? Not to mind; right is right and everyone knows it.

True, it takes more effort to lift others to one's moral standards than for us to sink to theirs. But nothing in this book is intended to imply that interglobal thinking and actions will be easy — especially short-term. Long-term, these standards made America what it was before the amoral social revolution of the recent past, when our world leadership began to erode almost as fast as our pop cultural morals.

Interglobal thinking is ethical and very long-term. We ethically engage in international commerce. We concurrently export freedom and democracy — until we have covered the planet in each of these important arenas.

But the interglobal mentality is more than historic, sterile rules of conduct overlaid upon the goods and services we peddle. Its essence is the pioneering spirit. This spirit filled the westward-bound wagon trains and put our men on the moon. The former Soviet Bloc is one such frontier!

The reader may choose his own frontier from the many presented in this book. "Being" is more important than "doing." First, let's "be" pioneers! The diligent, ethical "doing" will soon fall in line behind this grand spirit.

Rediscover this precept now, America. Time may be running out; the sands of time cascade relentlessly downward!

PART TWO

The Inward Look

Chapter Four

AMERICA'S
STRENGTHS

B
efore so important an undertaking as launching an Interglobal Age offensive, it is important to first count the cost. Possibly no discipline so adequately considers all of the pertinent factors as the strategic analysis taught in the MBA programs and employed by successful consultants and corporate planners. Therefore, the inward look, with its consideration of the strengths and weaknesses of the United States, will be the focus of Part Two.

First, we consider a select listing of our strengths chosen for their significance in the Interglobal Age.

MELTING POT

Alone, America has chosen to allow up to a million people a year to immigrate from a multitude of nations and ethnic and language groups. The melting pot has worked! The genetic, ethnic, and social diversity of this nation is unparalleled: we are enriched. Citizens of the U.S. can pick and choose the best from many cultures, just as we have learned to enjoy the best from a wide array of ethnic foods available in all of our cities.

This unique diversity is a great strength. For instance, as President George Bush spoke on July 10, 1989 to the newly elected officials of Poland, eight hundred thousand Polish-Americans in Warsaw's sister-city, Chicago, watched eagerly. A seldom-made point regarding the melting pot is this: it gives us an international outlook and dynamic unmatched by other world powers. Japan, the nations of Europe, and the former Soviet Union do not have millions of persons aware of their cultural history along with a strong personal interest in the well-being of the people in that nation across the globe. Thus, in spite of our geographic isolation, we have a built-in protection against international political inactivity.

LAND

"Oklahoma! Plenty of room to shoot a gun!"
— Rogers and Hammerstein.

Although many of the newcomers began their melting pot experience in the ethnic ghettoes of our great cities, they often migrated to the forests and plains. Unlike the most recent historic world power, the United Kingdom, and the present contender, Japan, we do not need to import great quantities of our raw materials and process them in cramped quarters. However, we are free to import those things that make us more competitive and that better satisfy our lifestyles. Folks in the American West tend to have a great appreciation of their "elbow room." Common wisdom today says that scientists perform best in research parks that have areas of green space and that provide quiet places for contemplation — space that is a luxury in many of the older, more populated regions of our world.

CAPITAL

Japanese banks have recently begun to dominate the list of the ten largest banks in the world. But this is not the best indicator of relative pools of capital available for business expansion. Our financial strength can best be seen in the balance sheets of local and regional banks across this enterprising land — where the small businesses make their deposits. America has a vast supply of capital for well-conceived projects abroad. Both venture capital and loan capital sources continue steady increases.

LIBERAL DEMOCRACY

We have seen that democracy is a relatively recent invention in government. Among the democracies, our two-party system has clear advantages. One party always has the upper hand in each house of the Congress and in the administrative branch of our system. There is no need for making concessions to splinter minority parties, which often have a destabilizing impact. This is in addition to the wisdom of the founding fathers, who recognized the frailties of human nature by establishing checks and balances within our government. We have been favored: small, new movements have been forced to work within one of the existing parties and to seek, if possible, to bring about change from within that party. Radical, poorly conceived changes have in this way usually been avoided. The wheels in America have ground slowly, but finely. And fairly.

FREEDOM TO FAIL

While much has been written about the "pursuit of happiness," the clearest distinction between socialistic nations and America, in the mind of many entrepreneurs, is the opportunity to try and to fail — and to learn from that failure. We are willing to forego security for this opportunity. Conversely, there was a standing joke among Soviet citizens, "We pretend to work and they pretend to pay us."

In practice, this "cradle to the grave" socialism has resulted in subsistence slavery for most of the people. A successful American businessman, who had failed several times before finally succeeding, on the other hand, remarked, "I know a lot of things that won't work, but only one that does." Yes, in America there are great opportunities, the greatest of which may be the opportunity to learn from one's own mistakes.

Sociologist Tom Smith, of the National Research Center, defines this American distinction as an "Opportunity Society," which contrasts with citizens polled in some other industrialized nations who form a "Security Society."

America has more entrepreneurs than any other nation. And we have more potential entrepreneurs; people dreaming of leaving the security of their job in order to prove that they can make it on their own. Have we a greater strength? Yes!

Most of these fledgling enterprises fail. So what? Lessons are learned for a lifetime. Some learn to be better employees on their next job. Others try again. But not all fail. Small businesses, not Fortune 500 giants, provide the new jobs in the United States. And much of this vitality comes from start-ups!

FAITH

Marshall and Manuel, in *The Light and the Glory*, have chronicled the secularization of America. Faith in God propelled many of our founding groups out of Europe. In recognition of this fact, President Bush, in July 1989, visited the site of the departure of the *Mayflower* for the New World, a first for a president of the United States. Their book also details the missionary motivation of the discovery of this hemisphere by a man named Christopher

("Christ-bearer") Columbus. When he first set foot on dry ground, he named the island San Salvador (Holy Savior) and prayed:

> *O Lord, almighty and everlasting God, by Thy holy Word*
> *Thou hast created heaven and the earth, and the sea;*
> *blessed and glorified be Thy Name, and praised be Thy*
> *Majesty, which hath deigned to use us, Thy humble*
> *servants, that Thy holy Name may be proclaimed in this*
> *second part of the earth.*

At each stop of his first journey, Columbus had a large cross erected "as a token of Jesus Christ our Lord, and in honor of the Christian faith."

The United States is still the most religious of the industrialized nations. Sociologist Seymore Lipset says one reason we feel that way is because church attendance and membership have always been voluntary, separated from government. Surveys show this: Americans are more likely to believe in Heaven, Hell, Christ, and Satan than are Europeans; sixty-five percent of us believe in a personal God, compared with thirty-one percent of the Englishmen and less than twenty percent of the Swedes, where citizens are born into membership in the State church.

One practical side of this faith is the ability to focus on the needs of others. Jesus commanded his disciples, "Whoever wants to be first must be a slave of all."

A GIVING ATTITUDE

The strengths of America are often the opposites of the qualities exemplified by Warlord Sun Tzu, who proposed that it is more blessed to receive — even grab — than to give. We have always been slow to be provoked into a war; we have been quick to forgive and aid any nation that chose to attack us. Germany and Japan must testify to this fact. We continue to be a blessing to millions in less fortunate nations, by our public and private programs of all kinds.

The warlords around us see this generosity as a sign of weakness that may ultimately lead to the collapse of our nation. However, they reckon, without understanding, the basic tenets of our Judeo-Christian heritage or the force of the words, "It is more blessed to give than to receive."

LESS CLASS CONSCIOUSNESS

While we are far from being a classless society, recent surveys indicate we are only half as prone as the British to vote on the basis of our economic status. We believe in upward mobility; we even have recently practiced some downward mobility without undue stigma. For instance, in the 1980s and 1990s, hundreds of thousands of middle management jobs were eliminated due to competitive pressures. Many, if not most, did not find comparable employment elsewhere. Yet they continued to move in the same circle of friends, at least for the most part.

AMERICANS LIKE TO WORK

Half of the Americans surveyed said this: they get a feeling of accomplishment from their work. Only about a quarter of the Europeans felt they were doing more than just earning a living.

INNOVATION

Why are we the most spied-upon nation in the history of this planet? It is not because we spend the largest percent of either our public or private revenues on research and development. Some television preachers tell us our greater creativity springs from a faith in God, and from a freedom from fear, which stultifies workers in the communist lands.

PATRIOTISM

Eighty percent of Americans say they are very proud to be an American — twice the all-European average and about four times the percentage of West Germans, who before unification, expressed pride in their nationality. Seventy percent of our citizens say they are willing to fight for their country. The European average is forty-three percent. Only twenty-two percent of the Japanese surveyed said they would fight for their homeland.

WE ARE WHAT THE WORLD IS BECOMING

America is a melting pot of ethnic peoples organized in a pluralistic free-market democracy. We are the envy of the world — and the model.

Chapter Five

AMERICA'S WEAKNESSES

P ogo, the inimitable comic strip character, often stated with great profundity, *"We have met the enemy and he is us."* A Gallup poll released in August, 1989 indicated that the American people see drug abuse as our greatest problem. They favor an all-out war against this menace. People are so disturbed that three-fourths of all teenagers and nearly half of all adults are ready to volunteer to help in drug prevention programs, according to George H. Gallup.

"In the fifty years that the U.S. public has been asked to name the most important issue facing the nation, it is unprecedented for any social issue to appear at the top of the list," Gallup said at a White House press conference.

Drugs were not a problem in America thirty years ago. Crime rates were only a fraction of the current levels. The national debt was under control; we exported more than we imported; we led the world in almost everything worthwhile.

What has happened? The robbers used to be on the outside of the banks and Wall Street. Thrift, not debt, was a virtue. People earned money the old-fashioned, hard way, not by manipulating the market for the control of a company in a hostile take-over bid. A day's wages bought a day's work. Wage-earner and capitalist alike prudently lived within their means.

What, indeed? As an immigrant from Hong Kong, I arrived just in time to see the fearful panorama of change unfurl before my eyes! The Asian mind-set, often inscrutable to the Occidental, discerns a single, sinister root cause. The weaknesses that have overtaken this great culture in so short a time are from one source: a youth-led social revolution.

From time immemorial, no civilization, great or small, has allowed its young people to rebel against its elders, family values, established morals, and religion. Never in history have sodomy, divorce, abortion, murder, and rape been allowed by those in authority to conquer a generation of young people. In America, the unthinkable began to happen in the 1950s with the advent of rock'n roll music, youth rebel heroes, and an assault on the cornerstone of society, the home. All proper authorities were held up for attack.

It is true that empires have crumbled because of moral decay; indeed, it has been the norm. But adults — national leaders — have led the way. And never has the decline been so rapid. Never has a religion of instant self-gratification mushroomed so quickly. Today, this new, evil self-worship has been exported to much of the world.

All cultures have recognized this truth: wisdom comes with age; in China, the aged are venerated. Yet America has exalted youth and tends to discard the older people, who, thanks to scientific advances, are becoming quite numerous. Should the reader doubt that such a revolution has occurred, he should ask someone reared in Asia to spend a couple of hours with him observing parent-child interactions in the neighborhood supermarkets, toy stores, and children's apparel stores.

History tells us that empires usually crumble from internal weaknesses. The American empire has become infected by the greatest of all weaknesses: a countercultural revolution, which now reaches maturity in devil worship and blood sacrifice. A revolution that set out to destroy religion is becoming increasingly cultic and intrigued by the supernatural.

To the Chinese mystic, there is no such thing as a void of religion. Everyone has faith in something: the Communist in his manifesto; the atheist in man; the American cultural revolutionist in himself. Confucius and Solomon, two of this world's wisest men, extolled unselfishness. The young American rebels have been permitted to seek meaning and pleasure in all the ways proven wrong and meaningless by the wise men — all the wise men — of the past three thousand years!

The list of the symptoms of this religion of self-love is long; a few prime examples are cited below simply by way of illustration.

DRUGS

Illicit drug sales consume hundreds of billions of dollars and have addicted half a million American citizens. Not since the British perpetrated opium addiction on a decaying Chinese dynasty in the heyday of colonialism has international drug trading been such a lucrative and corrupting business.

DIVISIONS

We are a dualistic society — partly committed to historic values that brought us greatness, and partly to an unseen, evil movement bent on national suicide. Enmity between the two has increased with recent Supreme Court decisions involving the desecration of the flag as a legal form of protest and the right to destroy unborn citizens by abortion. The issue of prosecution and imprisonment of drug vendors and users versus the legalization of drugs is expected to further exacerbate the rift between these two value systems.

Pluralism was listed as a strength; it also can provide impetus for positive change in response to shifts in the environment. But its dark side is black indeed: race riots, looting, shooting, gang wars, and old-fashioned bigotry.

An American educator who recently had interviewed Russian students returning from a cultural exchange with one of our universities sadly concluded, "The two main things they came back with were stories about our street people and our cuss words." Much of what they had been told about America, especially in past years, was misinformation, but street people *can* be seen on any day — in any city.

Street people have increased exponentially since the onset of the youth revolution, a revolution now mature and permeating all of our society. Democracy and private enterprise — can we in our freedom and wealth tolerate a blot on our good name, such as the street people? Have both freedom and free enterprise grown so selfish that we only take care of ourselves?

DEBT

The 1980s have been termed the age of avarice. The American expectation of ever-increasing consumerism ran headlong into global economic realities. Women entered the work force in increasing numbers. Second jobs became commonplace.

Personally, corporately, and nationally we plunged into debt as if there were no tomorrow. Corporate debt grew at the rate of twenty billion dollars per year in the 1960s; by the late 1980s it was increasing at about ten times that rate. One entire financial sector of the American economy had to be bailed out by the federal government. Commercial banks are in the process of writing off and restructuring one hundred billion to two hundred billion dollars in foreign debts and bad real estate loans.

The lure of high interest rates for the financing of speculative leveraged buyouts in the 1980s introduced twin diseases to plague the economy: excessive debt and inflated stock prices. When my column in the *South China Morning Post* on May 7, 1987 projected that the *DJA* would climb from the 1400 level to over 2000 in the not-too-distant future, conservative readers remembered this: the average had been below 1000 in the recent past.

EDUCATIONAL LAG

Many Chinese children begin learning the English language in the fourth grade. Their leaders are firmly convinced that their educational system and massive population will ultimately put them ahead of America. The Japanese high school graduate corresponds to the American junior college graduate. Because American educators have catered to the young "selflings," our standards are lax. We are functionally illiterate in geography. A foreign language often is not required short of the doctoral degree, in spite of international competition, which snowballs each year. Fortunately, we are finally admitting we have an educational problem.

LACK OF PLANNING

The U.S. continues importing massive amounts of crude oil and strategic minerals rather than stockpiling and developing alternative sources to keep itself independent from foreign sources. With regard to strategic metals, our nation is well able to build a ten-year stockpile in order to maintain its defensive position in the event these materials are cut off by the normal suppliers, primarily South Africa.

America, with its vast agricultural resources, has failed to make provision for a strategic reserve in the event of reduced outputs due to war, economic, or climatological problems. Since 1978, world food production of grain and soybeans has failed to keep up with the ninety-million-persons-per-year world population increase, resulting in drastically reduced supplies. At the end of the 1993 marketing year, world food grain supplies will be only equal to three to five months' consumption. During the farm-crisis years of the early 1980s, we easily could have developed strategic grain reserves for aiding developing nations as a hedge against devastating shortages.

America could be accused of living in a fool's paradise just for importing forty-five percent of its crude oil, a commodity largely in the hands of nations in the volatile Middle East. In fact, John H. Lichtblaum, in his book, *The Oil Market in the 1990s*, asserts that the combined effect of increasing consumption and dwindling reserves in the rest of the world will place the Arab nations of Saudi Arabia, Iraq, The United Arab Emirates, and Kuwait squarely in the driver's seat of the OPEC cartel by the middle of the '90s decade. Yet, the United States fails to even seriously consider an alternative energy program. Wake Up! Oil is a finite resource.

When its folly in strategic minerals, grains, and oil is considered, one can only conclude that our nation is seriously planning about as far ahead as are its corporate managers, who seem only to consider quarterly and annual earnings — to the detriment of long-term development and growth.

Another aspect of our short-sightedness — a tragic example — is our failure to bring our creativity to fruition. The Japanese are famous for being able to develop commercial products and bring them to the world market. All too often, the creative idea and the basic research originated in the United States.

Why did we fail to monetize our new ideas? Investors and marketers were not interested. Why take a chance, go to a lot of hard work, and wait years for a pay-out, they say. Even most venture capital funds have become impatient, now wanting to buy in only after products, sales, and profits are clearly visible.

The Japanese see us as having the same problem as Adoo Annie, who sang in *Oklahoma*, "I'm just a girl who can't say no." So says Sony corporation's chairman, Akio Morita, in his book, *A Japan That Can Say No.*

Perceptive Americans living in Japan know all too well the pervading attitude of derision most Japanese privately have for Americans. They see us as soft, selfish, undisciplined, and inept. Akio and his collaborator, Shintaro Ishihara, conclude that there is "no hope for the United States."

Are they correct in this stern judgment? Maybe so, unless many of the trends of the '80s are reversed.

UNBRIDLED GREED

"The worst fraud scandal in our history," described the U.S. Attorney General in December, 1989 as he dispatched hundreds of additional FBI agents and auditors to pursue savings and loan megacrooks. Megacrooks, indeed! White collar megacrooks, while complaining about "excessive government banking regulations," with malice and careful forethought drained a cool one hundred billion dollars in cash from deposits in their institutions.

If we can't trust our bankers, who after all dress and talk so conservatively, whom can we trust?

Over a thousand banks failed during the 1980s in the United States — a third of them wheeling, dealing Texans. Almost as many savings and loan institutions were closed by federal regulators: 804.

BEYOND GREED

Meg Harper and other graduate assistants teaching freshman English at the University of North Carolina gave students a choice: would they rather let the hungry of the world starve, or would they be willing to lower their living standards (driving a Chevy instead of a BMW, for instance). Almost without exception the young essayists chose to let the out-of-sight people die! Indeed an ugly meanness that goes beyond greed — far beyond.

PUBLIC CORRUPTION

The 1989 United States Department of Housing and Urban Development scandal can only be described as incredible, giving the private-sector savings and loan scams real competition for the sleazy '80s "fraud of the decade" award.

Most newspapers try to feature an upbeat story on the front page of their Christmas Eve editions. But it was no living nativity story that the Dallas *Times Herald* ran on that day in 1989:

> It was around last Christmas that one homeowner in stylish Waterwood Estates realized Reba Louise Lovell was a cut above the other conspicuous consumers in the neighborhood. He watched in awe as Lovell returned home from a holiday shopping expedition trailed by two taxis carrying gifts she couldn't fit in her red Corvette.
>
> "She was buying stuff, but she didn't have any place to put it," said the man, who asked that his name not be used. "I've made and lost a lot of money in my life, but I've never even considered living that lifestyle."
>
> Lovell acquired many of the finer things in life. Over the months, she bought the Waterford home, furnishings, a $12,000 Rolex watch and three cars. She also invested heavily, including in a racing-car venture that produced the top team in the world of sprint cars.
>
> Her secret was her benefactor: the federal government.

Last summer, a federal grand jury indicted Lovell on 79 charges, accusing her of embezzling $2.5 million from the U.S. Department of Housing and Urban Development in just four months, then laundering it. She faced astounding penalties: more than $25 million in fines and 1,030 years in prison.

Lovell, 36, pleaded guilty to four of those charges this month as part of a bargain with federal prosecutors.

Soap opera script writers take note: with the downsizing of the oil patch in Dallas, "Robin-HUD" scenarios may be the order of the day.

ISOLATIONISM

The ignorance of American students with respect to geography has been well publicized. We are headed down a dead-end street named isolationism — a fatal path in the Interglobal Age.

Washington Post staff writers David Maraniss and Bill Peterson, on December 1, 1989, told of student non-response to a colossal peacetime event:

One week after the fall of the Berlin Wall, Elaine Jester, a world history teacher at Kirkwood High School in a St. Louis suburb, showed an NBC News special about the cataclysmic events taking place in East Germany to each of her classes. It was such a compelling, emotional piece of film that Jester found tears coming to her eyes each time she played the tape.

Her students were utterly unmoved.

At McCallum High School in Austin, Texas, Jane Michael, chairman of the school's social studies department, taped the "Today Show" coverage from Berlin and replayed it for her classes. She told her students she had been their age when the Berlin Wall went up and that she would never forget how that symbol of the Cold War haunted her youth. Now, she said, the sight of it tumbling down released in her an overwhelming surge of joy.

Once again, the response was flat . . . "What's the big deal?"

The big deal is the Interglobal Revolution — without tanks and guns!

PARANOIA

"We have nothing to fear but fear itself." Winston Churchill, during the dark days of the Nazi aerial blitz of London, may not have been the first to make this statement; he certainly will not be the last.

Americans seem to be paralyzed by fear: fear of change, fear of loss, fear to act, and fear of the unknown. They are too often frozen in an inanimate state in government, in education, in the drug war, and in business.

Interglobal thinking calls for fresh, bold strokes in the face of the astounding pace of world events. And bold we must be, if we are to overcome our paralyzing paranoia.

Chapter Six

AMERICA'S
BOTTOM LINE

Not since the battle of Gettysburg have America's strengths and weaknesses been so delicately in balance — or her future so uncertain. After fifty-six years of sampling public opinion, George Gallup concludes that America always comes through in the clutch. His previously cited polls tell us that we are the only nation now emotionally ready to lead a freedom campaign. Or to constructively lead the global village as we enter the Interglobal Age.

ARE WE ABLE?

Many would agree that the United States has no business becoming seriously involved in exporting liberty and making a refuge for people fleeing from tyranny; no business in taking on the industrial might of Europe and Japan. Washington is slow in developing new strategies; our businessmen await its signals before moving into uncharted seas. But Interglobal thinking says this: "A good offense is the best defense."

Indeed, a recovery of the wounded soul of America outlined in the previous chapter can only take place by us lifting our eyes from our own problems and stretching ourselves into leadership in the Interglobal Age.

Our nation must carefully weigh the long-term consequences of ignoring the aspirations of other peoples enslaved by hardened warlords and simply concentrating on our own problems. History tells us we could muddle downward as Britain has done for the last fifty years, after having spent the previous two hundred building an empire on which the sun never set.

So be it! Decline is not irreversible. The great spiritual awakenings led by the Puritans, the Wesley brothers, and the Welsh provided the moral rearmament the British needed to continue building and maintaining their position as the world's leading nation at crucial junctures in their history.

Perhaps the dry rot, which subtly has been decaying our moral fiber, can be halted by the idealism of leading the development of the Interglobal Age — idealism of the sort that drove the Chinese students in Beijing to build a statue to the goddess of freedom. But it is an idealism tempered with a mature patience and practicality that preclude violence. And an idealism matured by a century of American-style private enterprise and democracy.

THE CHECKBOOK ISSUE

"Show me a man's checkbook and I will tell you where his heart is!" An uneducated lay-preacher in the hills of Missouri repeatedly thundered this assertion as he rode his circuit a generation ago. America must check its checkbook. We must reallocate our spending, as individuals, in business, and as a nation. The checkbook issue is important: it put Bill Clinton in the White House. Economic change was his primary issue.

The interglobal thinker will ask: "Is this a productive or an unproductive expenditure? Or will it just take money out of one American's pocket and put it in another's?" We became a world leader by allocating our scarce resources to pioneering endeavors — or more recently, to the cutting edge of technology.

Tens of billions of dollars should be prudently invested in developmental businesses abroad. Not in LBO's. Hundreds of thousands of us should commit ourselves both to career and also to relatively short-term employment overseas. Tens of thousands of entrepreneurs should plant both their capital and their lives in a worthwhile foreign venture.

The interglobalist's checkbook, career, and home are all on the line in the marketplace of the global village.

DARE TO BE DARING

"When Empires are Falling, Daring is Prudence." Perhaps headline writers should be setting the American agenda. This banner above a December 13, 1989 *Wall Street Journal* article by Albert Wohlstetter certainly gives us good advice. Interglobal advice!

There are no quick fixes to our debilitating weaknesses. The wisest man ever to live proclaimed three thousand years ago that there is nothing new under the sun. Solomon's adages are timeless.

"In a multitude of counselors there is safety," for instance. Yes, it is a time for daring thinking and daring action, but before a move is made, we must carefully lay plans in concert with able counsel.

Surprisingly, the interglobal leader also adapts some pages from the works of Warlord Sun. Detailed planning based on the best information available is followed by classic military tactics: resources are concentrated at the point of greatest opportunity and the element of surprise catches the competition off-guard.

And once project implementation is undertaken, management should post *Proverbs* 12:24 on the bulletin boards, "The hand of the diligent shall bear rule: but the slothful shall be under tribute."

This may be America's last opportunity to move from slothful to diligent and to exploit our entrepreneurial advantage.

Just Do It.

Interglobal thinking demands that we rediscover our creative roots. And nothing is so basic as finding a need and filling that need. The creative entrepreneurial spirit does not look for someone to ask for a job — he looks for a business opportunity. And not in the want ads. The truly creative among us spot a viable opportunity every month or so, and are usually willing to share ideas with the less creative who are willing to cultivate their friendship.

The principle is the same in the global village. We must learn how other people live and think in order to be able to identify the needs. In Hong Kong, for example, chicken wings are a delicacy. The same wings are hard to sell here. Americans prefer not to pick so many bones for so little meat. Yet a Chinese person from Hong Kong once exclaimed of the lowly wings, "There are only 2 on the whole chicken!" Small wonder that Hong Kong is now the largest importer of chicken wings from the United States.

But it will take a lot of chicken wing market niches to balance our ten billion dollar per month trade deficit. We must also develop new products for some of the markets we identify. Sometimes the markets themselves will be new, the result of our creative interglobal thinking. A few have immense potential.

For instance, the Worldwatch Institute in Washington, D.C. calculates that a third of global food supplies come from irrigated land. They further state that a quarter of all irrigated land is limited in its productivity because of the salinity of the soil. A small American company has developed a combination of humic acids and soil-borne microorganisms that quickly buffers these salts and restores the land to full productivity in a very cost-effective manner. Furthermore, the products can be easily manufactured in several agricultural regions of the world. University tests have substantiated their research and there is little competition. Yet the capital investment is peanuts when compared with most industrial projects of similar magnitude.

If the United States is to soar into the 21st century as the leader of the Interglobal Age, it must major in creative entrepreneurship — from chicken wings to vast land reclamation projects throughout the world.

PART THREE

The Outward Look

Chapter Seven

THE INTERGLOBAL AGE

The outward look at the nations of the world reveals a mixed picture: The former Soviet Bloc has partially opened to private enterprise and democracy; in some countries the warlords continue to erect whatever barriers they can to deter the osmosis of freedom; still others appear to be awaiting a push that could cause them to fall either way.

America is faced with its best opportunity, since the end of the Colonial Era, to lead the world in the Interglobal Age. Unfortunately, the enemies of freedom also have outstanding opportunities to take fragile democracies from a number of nations, such as those that emerged from the fallen Soviet Union.

We must be zealous. But, unlike the warlords, our approach must be straightforward and open, expressing a genuine concern for the needs of the common people. We must translate that concern into helpful projects. Thus, we can avoid the "ugly American" stigma.

But zeal and empathy are not enough. We must have an understanding of the people groups in this Interglobal Age.

FUNCTIONAL CATEGORIES

Most of the interglobal thinking discussed in the previous chapters has been rediscovery — forget the LBOs and get back to fundamental, developmental business. What the Interglobal Revolution has changed is how we categorize the nations of the world and how we do business with each group. The categories must be capable of assimilating the change that is accelerating all around us.

Interglobal thinking develops broad functional categories of nations — we call them "empires." For at least two decades into the 21st century, we should expect to see labor empires (nations with a significant pool of low-cost, hard-working people who would like to have a job in a factory). There will be nations moving up from a nondeveloping status to the labor-empire category, and there will be nations emerging from primarily supplying cheap labor to becoming commercial empire elitists, but business planning for the category will be about the same regardless of the nations that comprise this labor empire at any given time. Interglobal thinking relegates historic, geographic designations to secondary importance.

The advantage of the functional-empires categories is obvious: a farm-supply business targets an agrarian empire; the manufacturer of labor-intensive products is interested in the labor empires; and the vendor of sophisticated, expensive goods or services will initiate his marketing activities in the wealthy commercial empires. One Asian businessman wryly remarked, "Don't start your Cadillac marketing program in a labor empire nation."

The reader will quickly become aware that proactive interglobal thinking is not for the faint of heart. Nor is it for cynics like Carl Jung, who wrote, "It is becoming more and more obvious that it is not starvation, not microbes, not cancer, but man himself who is mankind's greatest danger."

KNOW THE TERRITORY

Too often, American businesses have merely reacted to international opportunities that have been "sold" to them rather than embarking on a systematic screening program. The interglobal approach is to take a brief overview of the world scene, then take a careful look at a specific empire and type of business. Finally, a detailed field evaluation is made of one or two prime projects.

The purpose of this outward look is to provide a background briefing for all Americans as we enter the Interglobal Age. The nations have been placed in unique groups that at first may seem strange. However, once this Interglobal Age concept is grasped, analysis will be faster and easier. Americans, take time to know your neighborhood: the globe.

"It don't mean a thing if you don't know the territory!" Peddlers on the train in Iowa sang this song as the curtain opened on Merideth Wilson's *Music Man.* A century has passed since the time of the setting for this delightful musical comedy. But the truth remains: know the territory!

So, count the cost as you read. And look for the opportunities — even those in working clothes.

The impatient may find much in this part of the book that he feels is irrelevant to his goals, objectives, and project criteria. Yet the wise reader may gain cultural understanding and precepts that could yield a million-dollar idea for an unexpected corner of the world . . . an idea that also will help untold impoverished people.

Considerable space is given to the issues of human rights and democracy. Rightly so: the eternal human quest for these off-the-balance-sheet factors was the driving force in the Interglobal Revolution. Open markets follow freedom as surely as the stars follow the sun. And we should never forget our moral obligation to the other five and one-half billion people in our village — the obligation to share these priceless treasures as we go about our business.

Chapter Eight

THE AGRARIAN EMPIRES

China is the planet's ultimate agrarian empire. Vietnam, Cambodia, and Laos are mini-agrarian empires. Westerners for centuries have called the Chinese "inscrutable." Vast mountains, deserts, and oceans separated them from the Western culture until the past three hundred years. The language, culture, race, and thinking of the Chinese combined to forge a cultural gap so wide that few Westerners cared to make the effort to really know *Han* race.

THE WARLORD

To understand China and her people, it is first necessary to comprehend that the peasant and the ruler are as different in their thinking as are the Occidental and the Oriental. Perhaps the incident of the training of the concubines by Warlord Sun Tzu can best illustrate the traditional ruling class mentality in China.

During the time of Sun Tzu, China was composed of city-states ruled by local kings or dukes. Sun concluded that they were highly inefficient at waging war. After careful study, he composed a thirteen-chapter book on the art of war, which he sent to Ho-lu, the king of Wu. He then secured an audience with the king, who asked Sun if he could conduct a minor experiment in the movement of troops, using women.

Sun said, "Yes," whereupon Ho-lu dispatched one hundred eighty beautiful women from the palace — his concubines. The king knew that this would pose a supreme test of the upstart's leadership.

Undaunted, Sun divided the women into two companies and put the king's two favorite concubines in command — one in charge of each unit.

51

He then carefully instructed his recruits in such elementary commands as "Front," "Left," "Right," and "Rear." The women replied, "We understand." Sun Tzu arranged the executioner's weapons to make it clear he meant business.

The intrepid young warlord gave the orders three times and explained them five times, after which he beat the signal on the drum, "Face right." The women all roared with laughter.

"If regulations are not clear and orders not thoroughly explained, it is the commander's fault," Sun Tzu courteously stated. Again, he repeated the orders three times and explained five times, then gave the drum signal to face to the left. More laughter!

Sun then stated, "If instructions are not made clear and commands not explicit, then it is the commander's fault. But when they have been made clear and are not carried out in accordance with military law, it is a crime on the part of the officers." He ordered the two unit commanders beheaded.

Alarmed, the king, who was reviewing the proceedings from his terrace, hurriedly sent his aide, stating, "Without these two concubines, my food will not taste sweet. It is my desire they not be executed."

Sun Tzu brazenly replied that he had been appointed commander, and when the commander is at the head of the army, he need not accept all the sovereign's orders.

To Ho-lu's amazement, the two women were executed. Sun commissioned two surviving favorites as his subordinate commanders.

Thereupon, at the signals of the drum, the women faced left, right, to the front, to the rear, in strict accordance with the prescribed drill, and in absolute precision and silence.

King Ho-lu suggested that the warlord go to his hotel and rest. He declined the invitation to inspect the troops.

Ho-lu realized Sun Tzu's capacity as commander. He eventually made him a general and his chief warlord. In that capacity, Sun defeated the strong state of Ch'u to the west and entered Ying to the north. Due in large part to the mastery of the art of warfare by Warlord Sun, the name of Ho-lu became illustrious among the feudal lords of his day.

The episode of the training of the concubines has been passed down in paintings and legend to this very day. From this incident, the Western observer can learn of absolute authority. The low regard for human life and human rights in this system can also be seen. So far, this is nothing new; such also was the state of affairs in the Middle Eastern and Western civilizations from time immemorial.

The outward courtesy of both the king and his commander in their dealings with people is an Asian distinctive.

Today, Western businessmen have great difficulty in understanding how they must deal with the outwardly courteous, inwardly obdurate Orientals with whom they attempt to do business on a daily basis.

A study of the teaching of Confucius and of the agrarian history of the Chinese civilization will show us how this courteous, even courtly, external treatment of others came to be part of the warp and woof of the Chinese culture.

THE PEASANT

China is a diverse country. Within its present boundaries lies greater potential agricultural productivity than exists in the lands that gave birth to great Western civilizations. Comparatively, the Egyptians had only a narrow Nile River valley suitable for agricultural development. Even the "fertile crescent" encompassing the area of the Tigris and Euphrates rivers was also relatively small when compared with the broad deltas of the great rivers of China. Persia was arid. Greece was both semi-arid and mountainous. Rome had a considerable acreage of rain-fed arable land, but its area was in no way comparable to the North China Plain.

The great agricultural area of Eastern China is most conveniently divided into North China and South China. South China, which is less well-favored with arable land, is well watered with monsoon rains. Dust storms are today a harassment and an embarrassment to the urban Beijing residents, but these storms have provided a continuous influx of fresh topsoil for the North China Plain.

Thus, the nation in 1993 is able to sustain an estimated population of 1.3 billion people.

Cultivation of these vast, tillable lands began about four thousand years ago. Maybe no other people on the earth have been motivated by their land more than the Chinese farmers. Families live in the midst of the fields that they have cultivated for many centuries. These fields never lose their fertility because the Chinese have known that where crops are grown, something is removed from the soil. Annually, as good stewards of the land, the farmers return waste materials and fertilizers to the soil. Each generation is responsible for maintaining the fertility of the land it has inherited, so that it may pass the land on to a new generation in the same condition in which it was received. One's duty in life is to respect the past and prepare for the future — an agricultural concept only about fifty years old in this country.

"Fields, gardens, houses, graves." This ancient saying signifies "home." Looking from this home, the Chinese peasant sees the surrounding fields and knows those rice and wheat fields grow the crops that will nourish his family and provide a cash income. He observes the little garden nearby where he grows the vegetables that provide flavor and balance to his grain diet. He sees the house of his family and neighbors and the halls where the tablets of the ancestors are kept; the graves on the hillside are those of the past generations whose labor made possible the fields, gardens, and houses of today. To the rural Chinese, all four of these qualities must be present if his dwelling-place is truly his home. The peasant, since before recorded history, has had more than respect for his land, his house, and his ancestors. He has reverence — a quality long since lost by the secularization of the West.

Since even after forty years of Communism, eighty percent of the Chinese people live outside the metropolitan areas, the life of China is still dictated by the mores of the peasant. China remains an agrarian economy.

The family is not simply the living group of father, mother, sons, daughters, uncles, aunts, cousins, and grandparents in the village; it includes the dead relatives, both newly deceased and the many generations of the past. Additionally, the unnamed individuals of the future have to be considered as an intregal part of the family chain that links past, present, and future. The living individual stands as an important part of this large family. His daily deeds and the character of his life can directly affect the well-being of his family. He thus has to exercise care in whatever he does, for the good of everyone. This excellent trait has provided stability for the Chinese civilization through long millennia.

Upon this sense of reverence and beauty, the philosopher Confucius, during the Golden Age of China, built further philosophical and moral foundations for individual life and government. Therefore, we see with the peasant farmer that the courteous, respectful treatment not only of other humans, but also of other life and the soil, is not a facade. It is genuine.

From the point of view of the king, duke, or warlord, this traditional lifestyle made the Chinese ideal subjects to be ruled. While giving lip service to the values so precious to the peasant, these rulers were often hypocritical. Outwardly, their manners were the same as the culture. Inwardly, they usually became cold, calculating, and cynical. This warlord trait today can be seen in business and government relations.

The tranquil, pastoral scene of the Chinese villages gave rise to a number of inventions, such as the plow and the suspension bridge. These rural Chinese were very religious people, believing that not only were the spirits of their ancestors to be venerated and appeased, but so were the various deities of heaven and earth. In some cases, even human sacrifice was practiced as they worked to maintain the fertility of the soil and to appease the wrath of the supernatural world.

More than three thousand years ago, the first Chinese emperor founded the Hsia dynasty. Many of the emperors sought to capitalize on the ancestor worship by proclaiming themselves as god-like and worthy of being worshiped. The cult of ancestor and emperor worship played a very important part in holding China together.

While the Chinese authorities often feigned the courtesy of the peasant, they were in many cases quite ruthless. The superficial courtliness of Warlord Sun toward both the king and his concubines, while blithely planning to behead the king's two favorite concubines as a method of controlling the others, is a cardinal example of the methodology of most Asian despots . . . including business despots.

In the face of often inhumane treatment by those in authority over them, the Chinese masses developed a somewhat similar strategy: they continued their superficial, almost reverential treatment of others, especially of those in authority, while masking their true inner feelings. Thus, over time, both ruler and ruled became "inscrutable Chinese."

An untold number of Westerners have learned, to their dismay, that just because an Oriental has smiled, nodded, and said "Yes," the person is not necessarily indicating real assent, agreement, or a willingness to take action.

Psychologists tell us there is something in human nature that causes people to desire a leader over and above the obvious need for someone to protect them from superior outside forces. Many people are willing to sacrifice money from their meager resources in order to take pride in the lavish trappings of their monarch, emperor, or religious leader. For instance, the Israelites mounted a protest against Judge Samuel, insisting that, like their neighbors, they be led by a king.

CHINESE HISTORY

Today, the Chinese populace are taught by the Communists to admire the dynasties that have been the hallmark of their civilization. They approved the construction of the new "Glorious Dynasties" banquet hall at the ultra-modern Jinling hotel in Nanjing, the seat of government of more dynasties than any other city.

Following the rudimentary Hsia dynasty, the old Shang dynasty controlled North China for about five hundred years, beginning at about 1300 B.C. In the late 1900s, the site of the city of Yin, capital of the Shang dynasty, was discovered.

The city had been divided into sections, each with its own group of special craftsmen. The city also contained large buildings and a court for the king. The Shang dynasty was followed by the Cho dynasty, which was to rule China for about eight hundred years. It was the Golden Age. The Chos ruled over a number feudal states, each of which was headed by a hereditary prince native to that state. In time, these princes became powerful and overthrew the dynasty. In 318 B.C., the Ch'im armies conquered the rich province of Szechwan. This gave its successors a base of further conquests, and in 234 B.C., the last of the Cho states fell and Shih-Huang-Ti became emperor. He broke up the feudal states and divided China into forty-one districts, each with its own military and civil officials. This strong leader completed The Great Wall of China in order to protect it from the barbaric people of the North and West.

Almost as soon as he died, there was a rebellion and the most famous and powerful of the dynasties was initiated — the Han dynasty — a name subsequently given the yellow race.

As the Romans were beginning their conquest of the Mediterranean world, the Hans were subjugating their historic enemies as far west as Central Asia, in parts of Korea, and south beyond the Yangtze River. Ultimately, Chinese soldiers fought Roman legionnaires where the two great empires' interests clashed for a short time. It was a cosmopolitan age! Koreans, Central Asians, Persians, and people from the fringe of the Indian Ocean came to imperial cities as envoys, merchants, scholars, and craftsmen. Romans were so anxious to obtain Chinese silk, jade, and lacquer that Emperor Tiberius passed an edict forbidding the use of silk in garments in order to slow the flow of gold from the Roman Empire to China.

One of the great accomplishments of the Han dynasty was the establishment of Confucian scholars as the leaders in government under the monarchy. These early bureaucrats believed that the world was divided into three distinct parts, each with its own function and responsibility: heaven gave light, rain, and was the place of the spirits; earth provided agricultural produce and other such necessities; and man provided government. These functioned in harmony as long as each carried out its special responsibilities. Obviously, it was unthinkable that heaven and earth would not do so. Thus, only man could fail in his government and produce discord.

The solution to this discord lay in observing the rules and the rights of mankind taught by Confucius and handed down from ancient times.

But the osmosis of freedom is timeless and universal.

The remarkable house of Han was toppled by the farmers of China, who were miserable under the ruthlessness of the military underlings of the emperors during the last century of the dynasty. Buddhism then began to be a strong force in China. Nevertheless, to this day, the combination of the earliest peasant philosophy of home and the teachings of Confucius remain the backbone of the Chinese culture!

The agrarian empire of China formed in the cradle of the fertile Yellow River Valley, and it expanded to the north and south by virtue of warlords and emperors conscripting the peasant farmers for duty and taxing them heavily. As the empire expanded its boundaries, and as barbarian forces from the north, west, and south became stronger, the pressure for military duty and taxation often became so oppressive that the peasants would revolt against the authorities. However, in general, the superior logistics developed by the Chinese with their defensive wall, canals, and roads, along with their superior military technologies, normally were sufficient to keep the various dynasties intact. Thus, the yellow peoples of China formed the world's longest-enduring state.

The stability and longevity of these dynasties is a marvel to Western historians. By what virtue did they remain united when the Roman Empire and all other civilizations collapsed? Certainly, it was not because the external pressures were less than faced by other empires: the hordes of Mongolia and Central Asia were successful in conquering large masses of land in India, the Middle East, and Europe. In fact, a common enemy, the Huns, drove almost to Rome at the height of their expansion. Internally, it is true that the Chinese had a vast agricultural resource that supported large increases in population, thereby providing a tax and population base from which draftees could be developed into citizen-soldiers. Additionally, the Chinese kept at the cutting edge of world military technologies. During much of this time they were, however, at a disadvantage to the horsemen of the steppes who learned to ride as children and whose ponies had virtually unlimited grassland.

Perhaps the overarching advantages enjoyed by the Chinese, however, were their Confucian governmental training, sense of organization, and the general respect for the maintenance of the peasant farmer at a level of income and life from which he would not rebel against central authority.

Alternately, Warlord Sun may have been the most important factor in the development and maintenance of this empire. The craft, subtlety, and deceit with which the ambassadors, agents, paramilitary and military organizations operated, were no doubt beyond comparison with their less sophisticated neighbors, who tended to rely on raw power. Surprisingly, this factor is usually overlooked by noted historians, such as Mark Elvin of Oxford University, who wrote the book, *The Pattern of the Chinese Past.*

A second puzzle to Western historians and economists is the cause of the technical revolution that made 12th-century China the most advanced nation in the world.

The farming revolution came first. Between the 8th and 12th centuries, China was transformed into its present farming patterns: wheat in the North and rice in the South. Better milling machinery led to the widespread replacement by wheat of the lower-yielding millet. The main area of progress, however, was in the South, where a completely new system of wet-rice culture encouraged a great penetration of this previously little-developed region. Revenues from the greatly expanded agricultural base provided the dynamic motor for economic growth. So great was this technological advancement that, except for the addition of chemical fertilizers, pesticides, and improved seed varieties during the past generation, little change has occurred in the basic culture of these two primary crops, of which China is the world's leading producer.

Agricultural productivity was increased to the point where the yields were far beyond the need of the farmer's family and his community — releasing a number of people from the land to engage in trade, crafts, the arts, government, and the military. The development of drought-resistant varieties that matured rapidly enabled the farmers of southern China to engage in double cropping. This revolutionary development in the 11th century almost doubled per-acre and per-man productivity! Thirteenth century agriculture in China was the most advanced in the world, with India being the only possible rival. Western medieval agriculture was centuries behind. This strong agricultural base allowed the Chinese population under the northern Sung dynasty to increase to well over one hundred million persons.

Transportation played an important part in China's development. The mighty rivers of China were natural transportation avenues; it is estimated that the 12th-century tonnage of the junks plying the Yangtze River alone totaled about one-third of the total carried by the British trading fleet in the middle of the 18th century. These vessels numbered in the thousands and were engineering marvels for their time.

Foreign merchants chose, when possible, to ship and travel under the Chinese flag. Roads and canals supplemented river and ocean transportation, giving China an enviable and unequaled transportation system.

Concurrent with these developments was the need for centralized monetary policy and banking, including the use of credit. A number of paper credit instruments developed. Deposit shops stored gold and silver for a fee; they would honor checks drawn against the funds by the depositor. Both they and the goldsmiths and silversmiths issued promissory notes that came to be used in lieu of metallic coins. In A.D. 1022, the system faltered from abuse; the government was forced to take responsibility to prevent a financial panic that would have resulted in a disastrous economic recession. The government replaced these private instruments with paper money. In 11th-century China, legal tenders were salt, coins, and government-issued paper money.

Market structures developed. Organization and urbanization occurred. The Chinese cities were much larger than their counterparts in Europe. But they were not centers of political freedom.

The 10th to 14th centuries in China were ones of systematically experimental investigations. The result was the world's earliest mechanized industry. The range of Chinese leadership was extensive: mathematics, astronomy, metal casting, clock work, medicine, metallurgy, fireworks, flame throwers, poison gas, fragmentation bombs, and the gun. The sciences of pharmacology and chemistry were also initiated.

With such a stunning array of developments, Western historians wonder why this civilization floundered and failed to produce the industrial revolution of the West. The highly respected Dr. Elvin suggests that the equilibrium between supply and demand discouraged further investment of time and money in technological improvements. A commonly held view is that North China was severely depopulated and disoriented by Tartar and Mongol conquests. Another cause was that 14th century China, like the late 19th century America, ran out of unexploited, virgin lands for agricultural development. Because of strong, competitive military powers, the Chinese foreign trade declined dramatically. The economy was denied foreign supplies of silver and other goods. The Chinese society had to look inward. Philosophers and scientists lost interest in systematic investigation, turning instead to introspection and intuition. Therefore there were very few advances in productivity in China from the 14th to the 19th centuries, a time when Europe blossomed and became powerful.

To a Chinese person educated in American universities in the disciplines of History and Political Science, however, it is apparent that there is only one real reason the Chinese industrial revolution of the 13th and 14th centuries did not proceed into one as great or greater than the one in the West.

The age of reason in the West gave rise to scientific observation, which spawned innovation, invention, and the industrial revolution. Such an age of reason and scientific observation of cause and effect had also resulted in the technological and economic advances of China during Europe's Medieval Age.

Unfortunately, just as China was in a position to build upon its existing technological advances to move into an industrialized era, the nation's intellectuals reverted to the mysticism of the past, and innovation almost disappeared.

It should not be concluded, however, that religion precludes scientific breakthroughs. In the West, many scientists have publicly acknowledged the Creator as the source of their creativity. Guglielmo Marconi, the Italian who invented wireless communication, is well known as a scientist and as a Christian.

CHINA AND THE WEST

It was, therefore, a stagnant, agrarian China of considerable land mass and population that was rediscovered by explorers and traders from Europe in the 16th century. From that day to this, the vastness of the Chinese "market" has fascinated the mercantile class.

In *China Watch*, John King Fairbank reasons that the Chinese date modern history from the opium war of 1840: "The opium trade from India to China was the longest-continued systematic crime of modern times."

Until this British opium trade began, there were few addicts in China. But Fairbank blames overpopulation, hard times, and corruption for the ease with which the big Chinese distribution network was founded and exploited to the point where many millions of Chinese were destroyed by the habit. From the current American experience with drugs, the easy route to riches by dealers and distributors could be added as a factor. This drug habit was disastrous for the old Chinese-Confucian way of life, which emphasized duty to the family and self-discipline. Thus, Westerners struck a mortal, immoral blow to the Chinese society at the outset of their intrusion in East Asia, and militarily, the Chinese were no match for the foreign gunboats and attendant troops.

Along with the opportunistic merchants, smugglers, and gunboats, came Christian missionaries. But the Communists worked long, hard, and effectively in convincing the populace that all the

Westerners were from the same mold — corrupters of the Chinese mores.

Early in this century, the Chinese adopted the Western practice of democracy by electing a national parliament. Sun Yat-sen became leader of this government. He was succeeded upon his death in 1929 by Chiang Kai-shek.

Communist ideology had been attractive from the outset to intellectuals in China because of its perceived anti-Western bias. By the time Chiang took control of the nation, the Communists were actively building their forces against the right-wing leaders of their nation. Thus, Chiang was faced with the unenviable task of fighting two wars simultaneously. The internal threat of Communism and the Japanese aggression were an insurmountable combination. By the end of 1937, these adversaries occupied the major cities of the North China Plain and the lower Yangtze River Valley.

With the end of World War II, the three-cornered struggle in China became a Nationalist-Communist duel. Mao Tse-tung found he had to make a fundamental correction to Marxism and Leninism in order to succeed in China. With more than four-fifths of the populace living in rural areas, it was necessary for the Communist movement in China to have the peasant farmer, rather than the laborer, as its backbone. The wisdom of this move has been proven during the past decade when the Soviets have been much less successful in feeding a populace only a quarter the size of China's. The Chinese Communists never forgot their rural underpinnings, although they did embark on ambitious industrialization campaigns patterned upon the experiences of the Soviets.

CHINA IN THE 1990s

China is afforded an opportunity to export its agritechnologies as the former Soviet Bloc turns to the basics of food production and as the developed nations turn toward more "organic" food-production systems. A Chinese scientist discovered a male-sterile rice plant. Subsequent plant breeding resulted in commercial hybrid rice, a technology that has been licensed by two American companies. Likewise, ecology-conscious scientists from around the world are adopting the Chinese practice of culturing insect-eating spiders as an alternative to hazardous insecticides.

For China, the long march to world leadership may lie in agriculture, the education of its people — and freedom. Hope for freedom presently is carefully hidden from public view.

Some businesses should be considering new ventures in China. Others should be negotiating deals, and still others should be implementing projects. There are many opportunities, but agri-business holds the most promise.

In just ten years, the peasant farmers of China have come from being the poorest class of people in the nation to being one of the richest. The farmers near the large cities are emerging as the economic elite. Those who cannot transport fresh produce and livestock to these distant central markets have received little benefit from leasing the land, since grain prices in China are set by Beijing at levels below the world price.

The Chinese Communist Party is determined to develop its own model for society, somewhere between Marxism and Capitalism. Economic changes are likely to come much faster than the greeting of freedom, however. The writings of Sun Tzu may be followed as closely as the writings of Chairman Mao for some time.

China sold itself to the West as an industrialized nation. A high priority for the Chinese was import substitution by producing quality cars and trucks (they only produced a copy of a 1950s Soviet truck). Two prominent European manufacturers bought their story and invested heavily in production facilities. However, these modern facilities were barely rolling vehicles off the lines in late 1989 when it became apparent that there were not enough cash customers — certainly not for two companies.

The truth is this: just three Eastern European nations, with a total population of less than one-twentieth that of China, have a combined gross national product greater than the Chinese GNP.

China is an agrarian empire out of necessity, since job one is to feed more than one billion people. This fact must dominate the allocation of scarce resources.

OTHER AGRARIAN EMPIRES

But China is not the only nation in the Asian agrarian empire; consider the other Communist nations in the same category. Vietnam, Cambodia, and Laos continue to live in the rice age. However, things are changing down on the communal farm. Capitalism is arriving. Peasant capitalism.

Communist China led the way in beginning to dismantle Communist economic systems by leasing farm land back to the peasants.

Laos, one of the poorest nations, has followed suit by giving communalized land back to the families that live on the land. This

Southeastern Asian nation is also emptying its detention camps, writing a new constitution, and revising its political system.

Among the Asian agrarian empires, Laos seems to have the best possibility of achieving freedom soon. Vietnam is perhaps a better intermediate-term prospect for freedom than is China, where the great leap backward of 1989 is running its course.

Argentina is an example of a non-Asian agricultural empire. Other strong agricultural nations include Australia, New Zealand, Canada, and Brazil. The European Community, of course, is a major agricultural producer and exporter.

BUSINESS OPPORTUNITIES

Interglobal thinking dictates this: Begin survey studies and negotiations in the agrarian empire nations now and avoid the rush.

Even though China runs a ten-billion-dollars-per-year trade surplus, she is tight-fisted. Therefore, creative financing solutions are often essential if deals are to be made.

One American agritechnology service company is negotiating a uniquely win-win deal with the Chinese ministry of agriculture. China's National Science Foundation recently proclaimed soil conservation and reclamation to be the nation's top scientific priority. Numerous American scientists affirm that the Chinese indeed have a massive problem. Fifty years of intensive soil conservation and land reclamation work has developed proven technology for us to export to them.

An American agribusinessman who happened to be in China looking for a project when this announcement was made began investigating the opportunity. He contacted the appropriate official, who confirmed his assumption that there is "no money available for implementation of a project."

Undaunted, the American talked with a number of industry and scientific people in the United States. As a generalist, he knew of the great need in China for meat, wool, and hides. He also learned that the Japanese were paying a premium in yen for cashmere, which is grown in an area needing reclamation.

Months later, at a luncheon hosted for the Chinese official and some of his scientists, held at an agricultural university in this country, the essence of a project was discovered — amid give-and-take brainstorming with a provincial Chinese leader. The People's Republic of China would each year lease a few thousand acres of eroded land to the American group, which would do the necessary engineering and earthwork, and seed the land to an improved grass seed of U.S. origin. The Americans would engage in animal production on the reclaimed land: the production of beef breeding animals for sale to Chinese peasants, and cashmere production. In this agrarian empire, the peasants have money and will pay a big premium for American breeding stock. The cashmere will provide foreign exchange to repay investors, while the sales to the peasants cover expenses in China.

The lease payment is nominal until the company has the now-barren land in production, is modest until the investment has been recaptured, then converts to a fair market price in subsequent years. Everyone wins: The Chinese land is reclaimed, their economy is boosted, American grass seed and breeding cattle are sold, and the investors should enjoy a favorable return on their investment, and feel good about how their money was used — a truly Interglobal Age project.

Most Americans view China as a labor empire, producing our cheap toys, trinkets, and trivia; but they see only the top of this great agrarian iceberg.

Agribusiness opportunities truly abound in the People's Republic of China (PRC). Surprisingly, it is even a place where technology can be leveraged without significant American capital. As has been stated, peasants were the first to emerge as the new economic elite: peasants have investment capital. For instance, one of the finest new hotels built in Canton in the past decade was the project of a peasant farmer. Management, of course, is in the hands of experienced Europeans.

Likewise, farmers and groups of farmers are eager to enter into ventures in agriculture and agribusiness with Americans because they know that whatever the shortcomings of this land of the free and the home of the brave, we do lead the world in farm technology and management. And the way has been paved by, among others, a large hog-feeding operation. In fact, animal feed, probiotics, animal feeding, meat processing, and meat distribution are among the better project possibilities. Biotechnology is another excellent industry for the giant Chinese agricultural sector.

But this most populous nation on earth is not remaining strictly an agricultural empire, any more than America remained one, even though we still lead the world in agricultural and agribusiness know-how. China, the most productive of farm empires, has in the past few years made the transition into a leadership role among the labor empires. But we shall discuss this matter in a later, more appropriate chapter.

And in the long term, watch China emerge into a leading commercial empire. For, you see, rather than China swallowing Hong Kong, the reverse is happening: the tiny British Crown Colony is swallowing huge China. The Cantonese people who inhabit Hong

Kong have already made an economic miracle of the area of southeastern China, where their people predominate. And the new rulers who came to power in Beijing late in 1992 are committed to make this section of their country a model for the whole of the PRC.

Unfortunately, these new leaders, while gradually freeing the nation to become more market-oriented, still talk the same old party line — communist control. Freedom seems as far away as ever. But is it?

Chapter Nine

THE RAPED EMPIRES

Warlords are rapists! Nations, not women, are their principal victims. Eastern Europe was ravaged for forty years by lusty Soviet Communism. The people of the old Russian Empire were raped for seventy long years.

Such inhumane treatment is nothing new for most of the nations of the region. Poland's greatest liability is its location between two perennial powers: Germany and Russia. Through the centuries, other warlords have raped the region. The Mongols. Waves of Central Asians. The Romans. Napoleon's French legions. Hitler's Nazis.

RUSSIAN RAPISTS

As the Russian leaders gained strength, they became warlord-rapists. The czars pushed south into Central Asia and the Caucasus and west into the Baltics and Moldavia in the 18th and 19th centuries. They brought under their control lands bordering other major empires that frequently threatened invasion.

With arrests, deportations, discrimination, and murder, the Russian czars did little to make the local populations love their masters in Moscow.

Alexander III introduced Russification — an attempt to make everyone Russian in character — angering non-Russian peoples. His son Nicholas II, the last czar, continued that approach. Soviet founder Vladimir I. Lenin called the Russian Empire that the Bolsheviks inherited a "prison of nations." In the early years of

Soviet power under Lenin, nationalist ferment was high in the same areas where troubles abound now.

AN INTELLECTUAL WARLORD

More than a century ago, Karl Marx became the first intellectual warlord. He should be remembered for three innovations in his chosen field: a basic change in the economic system, the abolition of religion, and plans for a protracted conquest extending far beyond his own lifetime. Thus, he was an ideological and institutional warlord, but a warlord bent on world conquest, nevertheless.

When Marx's dream began to become a reality in 1917, it remained for the more pragmatic Lenin and Stalin to develop the optimal systems for both conquest and subjugation of the prey. One hundred million humans have been killed and nearly half of the world was enslaved and raped. Warlord Sun would have been impressed. The world has never seen an empire so efficiently and pervasively evil as international communism — not Babylon, not Persia, not Greece, not Rome, not the Mongols, and not Hitler's Germany. None, ever!

However, in the 1950s, the monolithic nature of this empire began to fall apart as China went its own way, subsequently followed by some other communist lands. Nevertheless, in only fifty years, the Soviet Union vaulted to the status of a military superpower. It was her plan to use this power as a threat while using Sun's book as a manual in subverting and subjugating nations and people wherever the opportunity presented itself. But the inordinate emphasis on military expenditures created too great a strain on the economy, which, in the long term, was destined to fall or to be greatly modified because of the inherent weakness of central planning, the lack of incentives, and corruption.

STALIN THE RAPIST

President Franklin Roosevelt was ill, terminally ill, at the Yalta meeting of Allied Leaders. Joseph Stalin, the crusty old warlord, who had the blood of tens of millions of his own citizens on his hands, took advantage of Roosevelt's situation, the war weariness of the American people, and the inexperience of Roosevelt's successor, Harry Truman, to gain control of as much of Europe and Asia as he could.

Stalin had made deals for European peoples before, but Hitler double-crossed him! President Bush, in his 1990 State of the Union message, called 1945 a pivotal year. We lived for the next

45 years with the political realities established at the end of World War II. Bush termed the dramatic, largely peaceful events which began on June 4, 1989 "the revolution of '89" — a time comparable to 1945. It was Stalin who established the cold war realities.

Stalin wasted no time consolidating his control in the nations apportioned to him — some, such as the Baltic states, as Soviet Republics, and the Eastern European and North Korean lands as puppet nations. Might made right. Opposition was crushed. The Communistic system of enterprise was established. Religion was oppressed. Individual dissentients disappeared and group protests were brutally put down. As usual, the most blood was spilled by the farmers, who refused to give up their property rights.

Key East European nations were forced into military and economic alliances. The Soviets dictated the terms of both organizations. Little latitude was given the nominal leaders of the Eastern European nations.

Once-prosperous nations actually saw their living standards decline; average per-capita income fell to half that of the Soviet Union; indeed, economic rape! And the bungling, corrupt Soviet economy only produced an income for less than half that of our citizens.

While the economic rape of Eastern Europe was almost universal, the victims resisted the spiritual rape of the Stalinists much more strenuously. Encouraged and supported by the Roman Catholic Church, many Polish farmers never gave up their land. And Polish workers were given the courage to form Solidarity, an illegal, independent labor union. Lenin was wrong. In time, he thought, religion would be proven wrong and die out; instead, time has been most unkind to his intellectual theories. The quality and dynamism of Christian commitment increased throughout nearly the entire Soviet empire. Lenin did not study church history; suffering and martyrdom have always resulted in a purer and stronger church, which ultimately produces numerical growth. It happened in the Roman empire; it is still taking place in the Chinese camp.

But Stalin was no intellectual. His addition to communism was totally pragmatic: conquer, control, and rape. The warlords in North Korea and the would-be warlords leading leftist revolutions across much of the impoverished Southern Hemisphere remain his loyal disciples.

THE REVOLUTION OF '89

The osmosis of freedom was, for the most part, hidden from both the West and the communist overlords during the cold war era. Western observers had little opportunity for interaction and study of this osmosis; the communist masters were busy enjoying the privilege of power and the corruption that the privilege brought. These leaders were so detached from the masses that they were oblivious to the pent-up pressure for freedom, democracy, and the good life provided by the market-driven economies of their neighbors in the West.

The June 4, 1989 landslide victory of Solidarity in Poland in the first free election in the Soviet bloc was a watershed event; it was a great surprise to the Communist world; it sent a signal to all of Eastern Europe; it was a cause for elation for the free and for those longing to be free — it was a part of the initiation of the Interglobal Revolution.

What happened in the following months in Eastern Europe was unprecedented in peacetime. Never had so great a political change taken place without a great military conflict or massive subversion. The wildest optimist would not have dared to project such a scenario of change!

The real surprise is that a free election was allowed by the Supreme Soviet, whose members should have known that everyone longs to be free. The Polish election had to be interpreted as a signal that the Red Army would no longer crush freedom seekers in Eastern Europe. The events of the next six months proved that assumption true.

POLAND

It is only logical that the Interglobal Revolution would begin in Poland. It is a nation with one big disadvantage: it lies between Germany and Russia, two powers that have been prone to conquer the Poles every generation or so. Poland had been a fertile producer of potatoes, cabbage, and hogs, but the Communists turned her into a hungry nation. Unable to force all of the farmers to give up their land, the Communists saddled the hardy peasants with one organization to supply farm inputs and a second to buy farm products; both were dedicated to providing cheap food for the factory workers, a basic tenet of communism. The independent farmers almost starved. Yet they hung on, hoping against hope. "The indomitable peasant holds Poland's future in his hands" — this October 25, 1989 sentence by Barry

Newman in the *Wall Street Journal* tells us that their hope was not in vain.

Whatever the reason, Moscow allowed Solidarity to be on the ballots in a free election on the same day the classical Communists cleared China of student freedom demonstrators and Musavi Khomeini died — the historic day the Interglobal revolution began!

HUNGARY

But it took awhile for the importance of this day to become apparent. Nobody trusted the communists, be they Soviet or Polish. It must be a ruse, the people reasoned. But the ripple effect of June 4th did reach Hungary. The Hungarians, in October 1989, amazed the world with three pro-freedom actions. They ignored their treaty with East Germany by allowing tens of thousands of citizens to skirt the Berlin Wall and enter West Germany through Austria! A few days later they dissolved the Communist Party, replacing it with a new, Western European style Socialist Party — in anticipation of real elections with real opposition. And on the thirty-third anniversary of their violent uprising against Soviet domination, Hungary declared itself a democracy.

The world held its breath and listened for the roar of Soviet tanks.

But Gorbachev said that the U.S.S.R. would not intervene.

The United States responded by giving Hungary the "most favored nation" trading status, an arrangement denied by law to communist nations.

Gorbachev's positive response to the bold Hungarians opened the floodgates in Eastern Europe.

Osmosis gave way to an explosion of freedom!

ROMANIA

When the American colonies gained their independence, they were fiery zealots for liberty. It took less than a century for us to help most of our neighbors in this hemisphere break their European shackles. Freedom spread even faster in Eastern Europe. On December 21, 1989, when, true to type, Nicolae Ceausescu was slaughtering and beating freedom demonstrators, the newly reconstructed governments of East Germany and Hungary withdrew their ambassadors in protest. The next day, Romania had a new leader and the shooting stopped!

THE PROGNOSIS

Since warlords are rapists, we should look to history as a basis for developing a prophetic scenario for the '90s and beyond for Eastern Europe. South Korea is an example well known to many Americans who have been stationed there in military service.

Japanese imperialists began their conquest with the invasion of Korea early in this century. Their rape was complete; the land and its peoples were used almost exclusively for the benefit of the Japanese; the time of conquest, 1910 to 1945, was comparable to the length of Soviet dominance in Eastern Europe; even the forests were denuded.

Insult was added to injury. The nation was partitioned at the end of World War II. The more industrialized north was given to the Soviets for their alleged efforts in the Far Eastern Theater of Operations. The North Koreans and their Chinese allies, both with Soviet backing and blessing, then raped South Korea.

Wherever veterans of this 1950 to 1953 conflict gather, the conversation ultimately turns to the unexpected, almost miraculous economic recovery of this small, twice-raped nation.

The South Koreans and the Eastern Europeans are similar: they have rich cultural and religious heritages, they are industrious people, and they are not unfamiliar with industry.

There are also dissimilarities. Some of the nations in Eastern Europe have several major ethnic groups. The Communist system accustomed the Eastern Europeans to social welfare and the lack of incentive to strive for excellence, a system especially attractive to the elderly, the lazy and slovenly, and the addicted.

Certainly, the route to economic development by the new democracies in Eastern Europe will need to be similar to the amazing course charted by the South Koreans. They must first become a labor empire. South Korea's emphasis on education, especially at the postgraduate level, was a definite factor in its speed in moving from a labor empire to the coveted commercial empire category. Eastern Europeans, take note.

But the Eastern Europeans may falter when it comes to matching the Koreans' willingness to sacrifice personal gain to advance the development of their nation. Will they work as hard and as smart as the Koreans? — Another key issue that will weigh heavily in determining the future of Eastern Europe in the global village.

A substantial amount of foreign aid can be expected by the nations of Eastern Europe, cash that will be helpful during this time of painful adjustments and reallocation of resources. Some workers become unemployed as inefficient factories are closed.

Retooling, retraining, and relocation is sending shock waves through the economies. So, attitude will be of utmost importance. Government, business, and labor must keep a positive attitude — all through the crucial decade of the '90s!

The Balkan nations have a greater problem. Historically, the numerous tribal groups of Southeastern Europe have posed a problem for any government seeking to extend national borders beyond the narrow confines of a single major people. One example is the Croatian and Bosnian peoples in former Yugoslavia. The fierce nationalism of these various ethnic groups helped trigger World War I and led to intense civil war during World War II.

History repeated itself in 1992 when Yugoslavia fell apart and bitter bombardment of the Bosnians commenced. No one was able to mediate, nor dared they step between the combatants; not the United Nations, not the European community, and not NATO. Harsh rape of the various orthodox Christian groups by the Turkish Ottoman Empire between 1878 and 1918 was not forgotten. Rapee turned rapist with a vengeance, once the iron-fisted communist lid blew off!

INTERGLOBAL THINKING

Interglobal thinking says that Eastern Europe in the 1990s will be similar to the heady days during the first two decades following the close of World War II. Colonial powers were then being forced to give independence to people all over Africa and Asia; Europe and Japan were in a reconstruction phase following the horrors of the war. It was an unparalleled opportunity for American businesses to commence international operations. Eastern Europe is now in a similar situation, but there are two differences: the scale is smaller and the Europeans and Japanese are now formidable competitors for each business opportunity. And both have an advantage. The Europeans have proximity and historic ties; the Japanese have momentum. We should neither underestimate nor be overawed by either.

But make no mistake about it, Eastern Europe demands our best interglobal thinking and action. After all, it is the cradle of the Interglobal Age!

THE RUSSIAN EMPIRE

So much more could be said of the bloc of European nations accumulated by the Soviet communists during and following World War II. The task of redirecting their societies is proving

72

much more complex, difficult, and expensive than almost anyone thought, even for the commercial powerhouse of Germany.

However, let us now turn our attention to the empire assembled by the Russian czars. The problems in the heartland of the former Soviet Union are even nearer to being insurmountable than those in the former European satellites. Our intelligence agencies only saw the tip of the iceberg. The Soviets hid well their enormous internal problems. Mikhail Gorbachev, the first well-educated, knowledgeable Soviet leader since Lenin, was well aware of them when he assumed power in 1985 and began instituting liberal reforms, since he knew that the West had no intent to do his nation harm.

Before we look at the current status of the former Soviet Union, we should consider what Mr. Gorbachev was really up to. Jerry F. Hough, a professor of politics at Duke University and a senior fellow of the Brookings Institute, writing in the December 31, 1989, New York *Times*, listed three basic considerations that he believed to be driving Mr. Gorbachev's policy:

First, Gorbachev seemed to have absorbed a simple lesson that Western powers learned earlier: colonies are burdensome. Moscow has had to maintain at vast expense a large standing army to keep Eastern Europe under control. Just as important, Soviet relations with Finland, Austria, and even West Germany were economically and politically better for the Soviet Union than relations with Communist countries of Eastern Europe.

Second, he understood that his economy would have to be integrated into the global economy if its performance is to rise to world levels. There is more to this than buying Western technology.

Mr. Gorbachev wanted to compete with nations like Taiwan and South Korea in the export of inexpensive manufactured goods. He wanted massive foreign investment, and he wanted to solve the problem that would arise — repatriation of profits — by becoming an important world source of manufacturing components. None of this was possible as long as the West deemed the Soviet Union a threat.

Third, and perhaps most incomprehensible to conventional thinkers, Mr. Gorbachev and his military aides were talking about the revival of the wartime alliance. This, in fact, was the real meaning of Mr. Gorbachev's "common European home."

Gorbachev saw China and India — each armed with nuclear weapons and with a combined population of around two billion people — becoming superpowers in the future. He also saw that the West has ended 400 years of war and created a "common home" of 600 million Europeans, from the Elbe to California.

73

Thus, Mr. Gorbachev intended to move the Soviet Union into this common home so that it would become a part of a defense community of a billion Europeans . . . against the rising powers to their east and south.

Gorbachev, the pragmatic politician, probably years before June 4, 1989, planned to slowly initiate economic reforms and methodically move at least portions of his economy toward market orientation. But, ever the communist, he had not the slightest intention of moving as far or as fast as the Chinese communists have since President Richard Nixon made his historic visit to Beijing.

But the best-laid plans of men and mice go astray, or so they say. Gorbachev's did. It is highly unlikely that he ever gave serious thought to being deposed and seeing both the Communist Party and the Soviet Union perish. Almost overnight.

We now have a still-confusing array of independent republics, each mostly composed of a single major people. Most belong, at least in theory, to the Commonwealth of Independent States (C.I.S.). It is the Russian Federation, still headquartered in Moscow, that is the dominant factor — first because of its population, which is about equal to all the others combined, but foremost because the Russians control the vast majority of the nuclear weapons. Thus, Russia, after hundreds of years of conquest, has lost its empire, but not its clout. It is a military superpower.

Russia's economy, however, is in shambles. Reformation of the economy is not going well. The old communists refuse to let go of the power levers in government and industry. Some of the centers of anti-reform power include the military/industrial complex, which continues to turn out military hardware, state farm managers, labor unions, nationalists and radicals on both ends of the political spectrum (die-hard communists and the radical right).

The commanding heights of commerce, industry, and agriculture continue to operate much as they did before the hammer and sickle banner was hauled down from atop the Kremlin. The private sector that has sprung up displays all of the faults of primitive capitalism for everyone to see — including a very active Mafia. Things have only gotten worse for the consumer — much worse. Experienced observers recently returning from Russia say this: hardly anyone, even the young, any longer foresees appreciable economic improvement for themselves in their lifetime. The rate of change toward a market economy has slowed appreciably in Russia and most of the other republics — slowed so much that the journey to a market economy at the present pace will be a long, long trip.

What seems most likely to come to pass is this: within the framework of the present constitution and government, there will be a formal return to mostly socialistic principles . . . hopefully without the police state that went with them. Late in 1992 the Lithuanian people surprised the world by returning communists to power in a free election. Similar governments are gaining strength in the important nations of the Ukraine and Belorus. Even in Russia, the issue is very much in doubt.

So, what do we see in the offing for this huge, raped empire? A military superpower torn between communism and capitalism. This prospect does not provide much allure for most American business people, who are not noted of late for their patience.

What shall we call this strange apparition? Neo-Communism! And what shall we expect of it?

Well, suppose that a strong leader arises in Moscow or Minsk (the C.I.S. headquarters) and proclaims that the new system solves the problems of classic communism and classic capitalism — that neo-communism is the answer to the problems of the nondeveloping nations of Latin America and Africa. This line of reasoning can be carried further. Suppose he rallies the strong desire for empire that lies not far beneath the surface, and begins exporting this neo-communism. Perhaps, like Hitler, he would be a demagogue, and like him, would fan the region's already-glowing anti-Semitic embers into a wildfire. As with the Nazis, the charisma of a strong leader might be wondrously attractive to the populace that is presently trying to cope with its feelings after being raped for a lifetime and is concurrently trying to adjust to a new system that isn't working yet.

What would we call such a person? More than just a warlord. Should he arise, I would call him an Interglobal Revolution counter-revolutionary. A Contra who would be opposing every principle in this book. A Contra with 10,000 nuclear warheads. That's quite an ace in the hole!

Realistically, though, he would need to do more than just talk. The people are cold and hungry this winter. No problem for a demagogue; he simply focuses on helping the militant Islamic nations destroy their sworn enemy: tiny Israel. The scenario would play well with many of the sixty million Moslems in the former Soviet Union. Warlord Sun would love it . . . the odds are just about right. Perhaps he would raise some quick cash by selling mini-warlords a few nuclear ballistic missiles, thus forcing the State of Israel to make a preemptive strike at one of its overly-aggressive neighbors. Such an unfortunate situation might even provide him with a United Nations marching mandate similar to the one President Bush had for evicting Saddam Hussein from Kuwait. And . . . one last supposition. What if the Interglobal Revolution fizzles and somebody starts a trade war, bringing about a deep, broad, worldwide depression — which could cause a number of non-developing nations to buy into the neo-communist counter-revolution? After all, it is a lot easier in the short term to bankrupt our nation than it is to get out of our comfort zone and go out to toil in the Interglobal Revolution. But in the long term, such selfish, short-sighted action is disastrous.

Whew! perhaps none of these bad things will come to pass. But this one thing I know: there are always plenty of would-be warlords hanging around awaiting their chance. We also know that the exodus of hundreds of thousands of Jewish people is fueling latent anti-Semitism in several republics. And we know that nationalistic pride and lust for empire also are especially strong in the Russian Federation.

But the greatest temptation facing the Russians is their massive military. Compare them to a desperately poor individual whose only possession of any merit is a room filled with guns and ammunition. Then answer for yourself this crucial question: will they really be willing to scrap one of the most potent military machines ever assembled; are they willing to dedicate a full generation to gaining economic respectability when they are armed to the teeth; would they miss opportunities for expansion when presented with the challenge by strong, innovative leadership?

Logic, a study of warlord lore, and human nature all tend to cause us to answer this complex question in the negative. One last question before we leave the subject. Given the trend in American thinking since Operation Desert Storm, would they believe they have anything to lose by entering upon a bold adventure? Before you answer, remember that Saddam Hussein held a victory celebration when George Bush was defeated. How many other warlords celebrated more quietly? How many of these were in Russia?

Maybe you are now asking yourself this question: "Chee, why do you put such ugly ideas in the minds of the warlords of the Russian Republic?" Well, in the first place, they never cease thinking and talking of such nefarious plots, so I doubt that this is new to them. But more importantly, they can do just as I did, read it in the best-selling book of all time: *Ezekiel's* 38th and 39th chapters, to be specific. In fact, I understand that Russian pastors often ask visiting American pastors if this prophesied attack on Israel by Gog, who surely must be Russian, will come in our generation. Most respond that it is possible, but that it also could come to pass a thousand years in the future.

The moral to this little horror story is simple. From President Bill Clinton on down, we need to assume our rightful places as strong world leaders. There are too many warlords who are willing and eager to take our place — and none of us can afford for that to happen. Not only will the cause of freedom suffer, which may not concern most of today's Americans, but so will our economy.

BUSINESS OPPORTUNITIES

Recovery from the trauma of rape can be most difficult. Some carry emotional scars to the grave. So it is with the former Soviet Union. The situation may be even worse than meets the eye, since before these people were abused by the communists, they were serfs rather than landowners. So, in dealing with folks in the Soviet Union, one must deal mostly with people with either the mentality of slave or slave-driver, of serf or warlord. Neither is healthy, and neither is the kind of person with whom we are accustomed to doing business.

The Commonwealth of Independent States has more class 1 farmland than any other nation . . . by far. Most of their land is almost flat and they gave us the word "chernozem," which means black soil high in humus, carbonates, and fertility — the most productive major soil group in the world. Before the communist rape, they were one of the world's leading grain exporters. The communists alibied that the weather was too cold . . . or too wet . . . or too dry. Nevertheless, the great agrarian empire of old lies there, tempting us to spring into action with our dollars, technologies, and managers.

But since a conservative approach is indicated, beginning with retooling the people, the following program, now in development by an associate and a group of clients, is appropriate for approaching the vast, long-term C.I.S. agribusiness opportunities. Finding a viable business opportunity in the United States usually means defining a small niche. Over there, you find broad, gaping canyons.

The Soviets made stupendous blunders in agriculture. For instance, an off-the-wall guru in about 1927 convinced Stalin that genetics is black magic. In the same year, Henry Wallace of Iowa founded a new, small business to produce hybrid corn seed. Wallace became rich and Vice President of the United States. The Russians wondered why they couldn't match our yields. Another misguided citizen, who must have been a better politician than nutritionist, established the party line that protein in unimportant in animal feeding, so it mattered not that they couldn't raise soybeans in their climate. The result: meat shortages in what should have been an agricultural utopia (there are plenty of other oilseed crops adapted to their conditions).

The Soviet central planners were fair (if you discount unit cost of production and a few other details) at developing basic industries, such as the production of nitrogen fertilizers and the mining of potash fertilizers. However, they almost ignored logistics, distribution, and infrastructure. So, my friend has developed a low-profile scheme for beginning a business to fill this void. In the first phase, while survey and planning work are underway, potential key personnel will be recruited and brought to this country to work in one part of a fertilizer distribution business: transportation, storage (a year's fertilizer production is consumed in just a few weeks in the spring), agronomic services, sales, mixing, and application. Only when a cadre of C.I.S. personnel is suitably trained on the job will project implementation proceed in the broad, black prairies, which some have termed "the best single hunk of farmland that lies outdoors."

The new project must perform the normal functions of a large distributor/retailer of crop inputs. But it must also first import from the United States, then have manufactured where the mighty T-72 tank and other implements of war once roared off the assembly line, an assortment of specialized, sophisticated transportation, storage and application equipment — all of which we take for granted here, where vendors always seem to be holding on the other phone line to talk to prospective buyers.

In a land where for seventy years everyone was taught that it was O.K. to lie, cheat and steal for the benefit of the Communist Party, projects need to start with the basics. And nothing could be more basic than human behavior.

Thus, there is a wide difference between doing business in the two former communist powerhouses. Except for the decade-long, unsuccessful Red Guard movement, the Chinese communists never seriously tried to wipe out the practice of living by the precepts of Confucian philosophy . . . so that it persists today, with a thin communist veneer.

Therefore, let the businessman beware as he enters the empire raped by Stalin and his ilk. The victims include the ecology, the economy, and the citizens. And the hurts are very, very deep and painful.

Chapter Ten

THE
COMMERCIAL
EMPIRES

After the Soviet Union, the most prominent warlord nations of the 20th century have been Germany and Japan. Twice the United States has entered world conflicts to thwart the aggressions of the Germans, whom their neighbors were unable to stop. Japanese expansionism began about the turn of the century, after Japan was forced from isolationism by the West.

Ever the reluctant combatant and the benign victor, we assisted these nations in economic recovery following World War II. Both have responded by directing their aggressiveness to industry and commerce. Encouraged by the success of the Japanese, the "young tigers" of Asia have eagerly joined the battle. In each case, the principal objective of the commercial warlords has been the vast American market.

While these commercial empires offer their citizens varying degrees of democratic governments and freedom, they also tend to drive them with a materialistic nationalism. A generation is emerging that has known neither the horrors and privation of war nor the austerity required to build the industrial colossus in which they are living. Many of these young adults tend to react either by falling into substance abuse or by challenging the system to give them a bigger slice of the economic pie they are helping to create.

The commercial empires are important and they dominate world trade. The surveys previously cited show these industrialized peoples to be about twice as self-centered as our own culture.

JAPAN

One of the most successful races of warlords in history has been the Mongols, with an empire ranging at various times from India to Japan to Germany. The great Wall of China was built to protect the Chinese from these invading barbarians. Japan is a very homogeneous, mostly-Mongol culture. All citizens have fervidly thrown themselves into whatever banzai charge the leaders, who until recently were worshipped as gods, decided was appropriate.

The transition from military to economic conquest was an easy one for the Japanese; it was natural for them to integrate their entire society into an efficient organization for the assault on world markets. It all seems to have gone together for them with amazing ease. The efficient, hard-working labor force was happy to accept only small advances in living conditions in order to promote the national interest. Their best minds were trained to implement technologies developed throughout the world and to manage production and marketing in the most efficient long-term manner. They knew how to fool the Westerners with much politeness, geisha hospitality, and a never-ending array of business and governmental complexities. Thus, they were able to access the markets of the world while holding much of their own from foreign competition.

Prime Minister Uno arrived at the economic summit conference in Paris on July 12, 1989, ready to become the world leader in strings-attached aid to the world's less fortunate nations. Japan had also begun to repair some of the damage to the environment that his nation's headlong plunge to economic empire had created.

However, the Japanese economy appears to have reached its peak and may have joined ours in retreat. The economy seems to have some of the attributes of newly rich America in the late 1920s. Like America in the Roaring Twenties, Japan early in the 1990s experienced the unthinkable — their stocks lost half their super-inflated prices and an unrealistic real estate market tumbled, wiping out paper fortunes. The energetic Japanese responded to these calamities by doing what they do best: they launched an all-out assault on export markets.

Socially, the Japanese working class seems to be ready to participate in the spoils of newfound wealth. "Those who work the hardest get the least," says Hiroshi Takeuchi, economist at the Long-Term Credit Bank of Japan. Recent disclosures of financial and sexual wrongdoing by their foremost leaders are expected to exacerbate the trend of both blue collar and white collar personnel toward unwillingness to continue to fuel Japanese expansion at their personal sacrifice. Japanese war-lord-like leaders may have to contend with freedom seekers from within. The young Japanese seek freedom to be more like the rest of the world's young people.

WESTERN EUROPE

Germany to a degree shares with Japan a common Mongolian heritage; Attila the Hun brought that bloodline to Europe during the latter phases of the Roman Empire. However, neither the Huns nor the Hapsburgs were long able to unify Europe to the extent that the twelve nations were welded together on the first day of 1993. The Madrid accord assures that a common fiscal policy and currency will soon follow the market union. Many international business managers already regard this superstate as a *fait accompli*, and see Europe as the dominant commercial empire by the close of the millennium. Europe could pose greater competition to the United States than Japan because of Europe's greater population, technological and industrial base, and its diversity. The European Community is expected to be able to compete on more than even terms with the United States in its own markets and those in third-world nations. Like Japan, the Europeans have been very protective of their farm economy, since both powers recognize food production as a strategic resource.

George Bush was the unchallenged leader of the industrialized world. His departure creates a vacuum into which someone will be drawn. The present European leaders seem too preoccupied with their own problems to fill this role. Therefore, President Clinton has an excellent window of opportunity to rise to the occasion. But human nature causes people to concentrate on what they like to do and what they do well, not on what they need to do. Bush, in his administration, did not rise above the pull of this primeval law. He neglected domestic policy at the expense of foreign policy. It remains to be seen if Bill Clinton can assume leadership of the industrialized world. If he does, the commanding heights of world leadership are his, a leadership that could jump-start the American economy as well . . . he could lead us in the Interglobal Revolution.

Should the American president not fill this leadership void, a demagogue could well arise in the European Community to fill it. Remember this: nature abhors a vacuum.

Few Americans have thought through the long-term strategic implications of European unification. For instance, the E.C. has the potential to quickly become a military superpower. This is

81

particularly true should the Russian Federation and the United States actually engage in a major dismantling of the weapons, or should their Russian neighbor lose its military might through an unexpected defeat. The key question nagging those who read the history of Europe during the past 2,300 years is, "Will Europe be content only to be a commercial warlord, or will it again pursue territorial expansion?" History tells us to be wary. Under the leadership of a warlord, we could even see the resurrection of the Holy Roman Empire at the expense of freedom to many within its borders.

German reunification was unthinkable until the October, 1989 brain-drain flight of 50,000 East German citizens, the Leipzig demonstrations by hundreds of thousands, and the stunning sudden change in leadership.

As Eastern Europe recovers from forty years of being raped by Soviet Communism, West Germany and all of Western Europe can expect to be the big economic winners. Western Europe's industrial trade with the former U.S.S.R. and its satellites has been running on the order of ten times that of either the United States or Japan.

In the longer term, American companies must look carefully for niches they can supply in the vast Western European market. There are opportunities. Take cellulose insulation, for instance. The energy crisis of the 1970s caused our government to provide tax incentives to existing businesses for retro-fit insulation. Someone came up with the idea that ground waste paper could be blown into external walls between the sheetrock and the siding. A Borax additive made it fireproof. A new industry was born as more than a hundred manufacturing facilities sprang up across our continent!

Today, this small new industry is profitably exporting equipment and ideas to Europe, where the custom is to refurbish old buildings rather than build new ones. There are, no doubt, scores of manufacturers and service organizations who, like the insulation people, could profitably satisfy needs in Europe and Japan.

What can we expect of these primal competitors in the future? They have a fundamental advantage in their physical proximity to the vast Afro-Asian-European land mass, with three-fourths of the world's population.

Another fundamental advantage: they have not borne the expense of the cold war. They are highly solvent and fully focused on one Interglobal Age principle: business, not military might, is the business of the global village.

The European Community has already shown its most likely future trend. First, it began pulling its 12-nation, 325-million-consumer market into something resembling the United States of Europe. Then it signed a treaty with the 32-million-citizen European Free Trade Association — giving it a strong trading advantage over distant nations. The E.C. is now reaching out to embrace Eastern Europe. Suddenly, a 500-million-person market towers above the world. Should a radically reformed Soviet Union complete this "common European home," the population base rises to the size of India —but with twenty times the wealth. Europe, Inc., could also add a contiguous ring of North African and Middle Eastern nations to its sphere of influence. Yes, old-fashioned European spheres of influence — commercial influence, this time, with all of the Europeans pulling together instead of fighting each other.

Japan, Inc., of course, will likely concurrently develop its own Asian sphere in which it will seek dominance.

So, perhaps the century will end as it began, with Germany and Japan building spheres of influence — Interglobal spheres that tend to isolate the United States in its relatively sparsely populated second world. Only a highly-motivated American team will profitably penetrate these regrouping spheres.

THE YOUNG TIGERS

Perhaps Japan's East Asian neighbors will one day be so strongly allied with them that they will be considered as a unit; perhaps not. For the foreseeable future, however, we must consider separately the four East Asian nations that have quickly and well learned commercial empire building from their former conqueror and have with equal speed penetrated American and world markets with their manufactured goods.

Thailand now seems poised to join Korea, Singapore, Hong Kong, and Taiwan in the role of newly industrialized nations: the famous young tigers.

While they are not individually major factors in American foreign policy and trade considerations, the collective aggressiveness of these nations in approaching world markets has a serious impact on our trade balance. Unfortunately, the Korean farmers have also learned well from the Japanese soil people. Both riot at the slightest hint that their markets might be opened to American agricultural products.

Perhaps one of the most serious blows that the Japanese and their Pacific Rim cohorts have landed on the United States is the growing list of products, like the popular VCRs, that are no longer manufactured here. While we hope improved living standards in Asia ultimately will moderate our balance of trade problems, it will be difficult to bring back manufacturing of an item once all of our facilities are scrapped.

American business visitors usually feel comfortable in a young tiger nation. Communication is easy; many key people are graduates of our universities — often with honors. And theirs are business-oriented societies.

Yet, niches for our products and services are many times more difficult to find there than in Japan or Europe. In the first place, the market in each nation is smaller. Then, we find these nations have more small, aggressive entrepreneurs looking for the same niches we see in the larger commercial empires. Finally, there is the reality that these nations were only recently labor empires; people there make less money than their counterparts in Europe and Japan. Consumption is therefore lower on a per-capita basis.

Thus, opportunities are more likely to be found in the industrial and commercial sectors, rather than in consumer goods. Nevertheless, labor rates continue to rise as full employment is reached. A patient Interglobal Age strategist would be satisfied with modest initial sales, hoping for faster-than-average annual increases.

Technology transfer and machine tools should present some sterling business opportunities in the young tiger empires.

THE OIL EMPIRES

Alone among the commercial empires, the formation of an oil cartel has resulted in an empire category. The warlord mentality can be seen easily. Unable to defeat Israel, the oil-rich Arab nations of the Middle East early in the 1970s established the Organization of Petroleum Exporting Countries (OPEC). It was malevolent in its conception.

The cartel was most successful during the 1970s, then relatively unsuccessful in controlling prices during most of the 1980s. It appears ready now to be able to assert itself much more strongly in the ever-expanding world energy market, as domestic production in the United States and other non-OPEC nations declines, and as other exporting nations that do not belong to OPEC tend to follow their leadership.

From a geopolitical standpoint, the oil cartel wreaked great havoc at its inception, when it was able to raise oil prices from the area of $4 per barrel to over $43. While the world economy felt the shock of this unconscionable tenfold escalation, the industrialized nations were best able to cope with it. Some developing nations — Brazil, for instance — were turned into non-developing nations and have yet to recover from the impact on their delicate economies.

This economic instability in a number of poor oil-importing nations provides the enemies of freedom with prime opportunities for making trouble.

Americans, for their part, after a brief "energy crisis" flap by consumers, ignore the staggering drain on our economy. In 1988 we imported almost $38 billion in crude oil and petroleum products, second only to the $45-billion tab for imported automobiles. The Kingdom of Saudi Arabia, the richest oil empire nation in terms of production and oil reserves, is a semi-feudal state ruled by an absolute, albeit benign, monarch.

Sam Fletcher, *Houston Post* energy reporter, on December 16, 1989 covered an Arthur Anderson & Company symposium:

> Dr. Fadhil Al-Chalabi, a former deputy secretary general of OPEC, said he expects exports of Soviet oil to decrease during the 1990s, increasing demand for OPEC oil.
>
> Chalabi said OPEC's strategy of reducing oil prices in the late 1980s to regain market shares has succeeded. "The so-called volume battle was completely won by OPEC," he said.
>
> Lower prices, he said, have discouraged development of energy resources outside of OPEC, particularly in the United States.
>
> He claims OPEC's actions have stabilized the world industry — perhaps at a lower level than desired in this country, but it will never amount to a collapse.
>
> The real question, Chalabi said, is whether OPEC can increase its production by another 6 million barrels a day to meet growing demand for oil in the 1990s.
>
> Another speaker, Joseph A. Stanislaw, coordinator of international economics at the Cambridge Energy Research Associates Inc., said OPEC members are likely to turn to private oil companies — probably through production sharing agreements — to help finance the $30 billion to $50 billion they will need to keep up with the growth in demand.

A megaopportunity for interglobalists!

Smaller drilling and production companies are looking at some outstanding opportunities in places like Romania, Russia, and China.

Increasing prices and improving technologies should give Americans the chance to at last become major producers of alternate fuels.

But the oil patch has been feast or famine in the past. Our businessmen and promoters flocked to the oil empire nations as petroleum prices skyrocketed fifteen years ago. So did the Europeans and the Japanese. But as OPEC drove prices down to force out the competition, the opportunists departed.

This time could be different. Everyone is predicting that supply and demand will be in balance soon. Thus, shortages will be real, not induced by controlled production and marketing. The Interglobal Age approach is to move before boom-times return. W.R. Grace is already quietly buying up drilling rigs and drilling contractors who haven't gone broke and are now hanging tough.

Parker Drilling of Tulsa is operating profitably — thanks to management's being willing to go to unlikely places in the South Pacific and the Far East. Tens of thousands of companies in the United States may be faced with the decision Parker faced a few years ago: go international or go out of business. Interglobalists will learn from Parker, not from their competition who hung around the petroleum clubs complaining to their friends about the dramatic decline in the number of active drilling rigs in the United States.

Venezuela, our most prosperous neighbor to the south, invites interglobalists' attention as it attempts diversification of its crude-oil-driven economy.

THE DRUG EMPIRES

The Republic of Colombia and The Socialist Republic of The Union of Burma are both trouble spots. It is dangerous to live there. They have this in common: they are drug empires.

Colombia exports cocaine; Burma exports opium. Both substances are illegal, addictive, and cartelized.

Western nations long ago decided that cartels were not in the best interest of the consumer, and made them illegal. Unfortunately, this fact is seldom mentioned in the context of OPEC and the oil empires. Of course, modern societies also made trading and using these powerful drugs unlawful.

The destruction and violence of the drug empires spreads far beyond the borders of the producing and processing nations. The need to raise money to purchase drugs drives the addict to crime.

The influence of drugs can remove inhibitions to commit personal attacks, including murder and rape. In fact, violent crime rates in the American cities are usually good barometers of the degree of drug use. Washington, D.C., where the mayor was arrested for cocaine use, is reputed to lead America in both.

Washington. First in war. First in peace. First in drugs and crime!

The criminals are of two major categories: those involved in the distribution and use of the drugs, and those who transmit and launder the money. The number of dollars involved is so large that each of these activities can be quite tempting. How else can a young person earn $1,000 for a night's work? How else can a businessman or banker become wealthy in only a year?

To our credit, we have declared war on the drug spree. The President has declared that he will allocate whatever resources it takes to win this war.

Burma is not so united, nor does it have the resources of the United States (per-capita income is only about $200). Furthermore, there are private armies promoting ethnic dominance, communism, and protection of the drug trade. Because the nation has isolated itself from the world, thus locking the people into a hand-to-mouth lifestyle, the opium-producing area of the nation is called the "golden triangle."

Colombia is one of the most violent nations on earth: the government faces Marxist rebels, the drug barons, and rugged terrain. Its enemies have taken the battle to the streets of Bogota, so, as with many wars, innocent civilians absorb much of the horrors and live in daily fear. In spite of the obstacles, the valiant elected officials are winning battles. They deserve our support.

But are Americans willing to help, risking their capital and their necks? One enterprising group is. They are planning to help the Colombians cut off at the roots the drug supply by helping farmers who now grow drugs to earn more money by producing newly developed seed varieties to sell around the world — thereby creating a high-tech development and production center for crop and vegetable seed.

Interglobal thinking!

COMMERCIAL EMPIRES: FRIENDS OR FOES?

America is faced with two challenges in dealing with the commercial empire nations: we need a level playing field in commerce, and we need their help in making this world a safer, freer, and more prosperous place in which to live.

"Obvious, my dear Watson." Sherlock Holmes would have spoken this familiar cliche after only a brief survey of the present global village. The commercial empires have most of the wealth; they import most of the products; they are, therefore, the first place beyond our own boundaries for most American companies to seek profits.

Unfortunately for our business community, the playing field is NOT level — especially in Japan. Warlords have erected many barriers to trade; yet our markets have made them wealthy. And establishing a branch or affiliate can be even more difficult than selling a product or service. T. Boone Pickens in 1989 learned that American shareholders in Japanese businesses are unable even to become a member of the board of directors. Go Home, Texas corporate raider!

However, Yankee ingenuity can usually find a market niche and a way to monetize the targeted opportunity.

Yankee ingenuity! The precursor of interglobal thinking. It once made America a great business power, and in so doing, the undisputed leader of the world. Updated, it can do it again.

Chapter Eleven

THE LABOR EMPIRES

Global sourcing of labor-intensive products has spawned a new category of nations: the labor empires. The first thing to understand about labor empires is that a low wage rate is not the only criterion for membership. Many Latin American and African nations have high unemployment and cheap labor, but do not qualify. The workers also must be industrious and accurate. It is the unit cost of quality products that determines the suitability of a work force as a labor empire.

Then there is the issue of political stability. And, unfortunately, some nations with all of the above factors are not labor empires simply because there are far more unemployed and under-employed persons in the world than there are manufacturing jobs.

In fact, the world supply of cheap labor, with the present 90-million-person-per-year net increase in population, appears to be inexhaustible for businesses seeking least-cost manufactured goods. Some nations may need help in training their personnel, but this obstacle need not be faced in the short term. Cash customers, not laborers, are in short supply.

CHINA

Although China is an agrarian empire, it is also a labor empire capable of quickly converting a hundred million farmers into industrial workers.

America has, for a century, feared cheap Chinese labor. The Statue of Liberty is in New York harbor, not beside the Golden Gate Bridge; it welcomed European, not Asian immigrants. We restricted the entry of Asian immigrants during the same century in which we welcomed Europe's huddled masses. China was and is this planet's ultimate reservoir of cheap labor. Hardworking, skillful labor.

China, the nation that gave the world so many inventions before the Industrial Revolution in the West, has never long known democracy. But she has known dynasties, poverty, and exploitation — three thousand years of them.

So, most Chinese believed the clever communist propaganda. They thought a new day had dawned when, after a long march and a longer conflict, the Soviet-trained People's Liberation Army expelled the Nationalist Army. Four decades of cruel experience have taught them this: freedom is as far away as ever — perhaps farther.

The overlords in Beijing see China making a "second long march." Their longheaded objective is nothing less than super-power status. The points along the march are logical: from the agrarian empire to labor empire status, then on to the level of commercial empire and military parity with any and all other nations. The communist leaders see their strengths as a vast supply of $30-per-month labor, a strong educational program, and industrial development. These cynics regard the massacre of the student freedom advocates as only a minor delay in this second and longer march of their movement.

Nevertheless, the initiatives toward private enterprise in coastal and southern China are not being unduly inhibited, since this sector earns most of the nation's precious foreign currency through its supply of labor-intensive goods for the West.

Most persons in business in this industrializing area are not disillusioned or idealistic about communism. They clearly understand that the Communists are in control.

Therefore, in the prosperous Guandong Province, the business establishment and the Communist Party have operated under a tacit agreement that the government would not strongly interfere with private enterprise and the people would not agitate for democracy or freedom of speech, the press, or religion. Indeed, during the April through June turmoil in Beijing, there was not a single freedom protest reported in this rich province of Cantonese people.

OTHER ASIAN NATIONS

Other Asian nations are receiving increasing attention as sources of labor-intensive products. Most world-class corporations have avoided Africa and Latin America like the plague, even though the labor force in Northern Mexico has proven highly adaptable in supplanting American labor.

The Buddhist Kingdom of Thailand is fascinating to Westerners in that it has never been defiled by colonial power.

The nation has a constitutional monarchy with a popular king, giving it a strong and stable government. Chinese citizens, although they comprise only 12% of the population, are the merchant class and have been instrumental in initiating the industrialization of the nation and in the formation of a stock market in the capital city of Bangkok.

Thailand has fifty million people, with an average annual per capita income of under $1,000 per year, making it a favorite location for those seeking to establish manufacturing facilities in a labor empire nation.

The Republic of the Philippines has had less success than most Asian Rim nations in attracting foreign investment, joint ventures, and sourcing for industrial products, because of widespread corruption and the presence of a strong communist insurgency. This loss of international confidence in the country's future has caused hardship, rising unemployment, rampant inflation, and widespread poverty.

The 36% Chinese minority in the State of Malaysia also has been instrumental in developing industry and an active securities exchange for local stocks. Although the capital city, Kuala Lumpur, is one of the most charming in Asia, industrial interest is somewhat dimmed by the high unemployment rate, by the relatively high cost of labor, and by tension between the Moslem half of the population, mostly Malays, and the balance of the people.

Surprisingly, the new leadership in India is positioning that nation, with its 800 million population and low ($270 per capita per year) income, into the competition for world markets with low-cost manufactured goods, joint ventures, and new investment opportunities for industrialists. In recent decades, this subcontinent nation has developed a sufficient infrastructure and entrepreneurial base to become a serious contender in the global labor market.

Indonesia is showing signs of shaking off its complacency. Long content to rely on petroleum and its derivatives, this populous island nation is now actively attracting industry. Many of the companies are from other East Asian nations. Check out Indonesia as a labor market.

THE WESTERN HEMISPHERE

Mexico is making an amazing turn toward private enterprise. President Carlos Salinas de Gortari is properly concentrating his government's resources, which are severely diminished by debt service, on infrastructure. He had reduced his annual budget

91

deficit from 16% of gross domestic product to less than 4% in 1990.

The Mexican government is closing or selling some 770 companies; competition is coming to our next-door neighbor. And so are the North Americans. Chili's, a popular Dallas-based Mexican-style chain, is opening restaurants in Mexico City, Acapulco, and Cancun. Tex-Mex goes south!

Carrying coals to Newcastle! Bold and innovative, but not true interglobalism; we must orient our thinking to developmental projects that help all the people. Mexico may be making the transition from non-development to labor-empire. Other Latin American nations showing signs of becoming hospitable toward the private sector include Guatemala, Brazil, and Argentina.

THE FREEDOM ISSUE

It is difficult to chronicle the devastation that has impacted the United States and that will continue to pummel it, in the years to come, from these low-cost labor sources. Industries have disappeared; labor unions are crumbling; working mothers have become the norm. Living standards are declining in spite of rapid increases in the use of credit to maintain accustomed lifestyles.

Sam Walton became the richest man in America by recognizing the trend: the consumer needs to get more purchasing power for his dollar, and desires a supplier who supports American labor. Still, most American merchants seek to identify an upscale market niche and to profit from it. Long term, it will be the Waltons who will win in American merchandizing. Supply the consumer with the basics as efficiently and as cheaply as possible. A highly successful formula for the 1980s, an almost certain winner in the '90s!

America must use the leverage of its vast market to force progress toward freedom, fairness, and justice in its labor empire competitors. As these noble objectives are obtained, the competitors must then be encouraged to join us in exporting liberty to less enlightened countries.

BUSINESS OPPORTUNITIES

Aside from the obvious least-cost sourcing opportunities, Americans may also monetize their know-how. Labor empires desire to move into the twenty-first century as newly industrialized nations. Unfortunately, some governments — India, for instance — continue to throw up substantial, unreasonable obstacles to commerce.

Patience and positioning are the keys to profits in these empires. Patience — an old virtue. It can be learned by American businessmen. It must be practiced — beginning now.

China; indeed, the entire Communist camp, could be regarded as a labor empire because they have never developed a viable consumer-products industry. A unique opportunity to liaison with the Communist nations is in the area of teaching entrepreneurship, and in the provision of volunteer cadres of craftsmen to work alongside their counterparts to demonstrate skills, workmanship, and the work ethic. The Communist welfare state has spawned a generation of people who have forgotten how to work. By definition, for a labor empire to succeed, its people must be willing to work hard.

As Americans engage in commercial intercourse and interact in other ways with the peoples of Thailand, we can encourage an orderly increase in democracy. Likewise, in our relations with Filipinos, we can reinforce their democracy, while seeking to tear down their country's stifling corruption, by steadfastly refusing to give or to accept any form of bribe.

Obviously, the labor empire nations are of primary benefit to the business community in the United States as a source of low-cost labor. They also are a good place to market machine tools and the ancillary products and services needed by growing industries. And don't forget the need many firms will have to upgrade their facilities, many of which started on a shoestring. This often creates a market for equipment that is either surplus or obsolete here.

Because the labor empires are poor, the availability to finance a sale will often be crucial. The other commercial empires often have excellent financing as a part of their sales package. Carefully selected projects could have fine long-term results. Some of these nations are expected to expand their industrial base quite rapidly during the next two or three decades . . . and become commercial empires.

Interglobal thinking balances short-term and long-term objectives. Excellent opportunities to do this now appear to abound in the labor-empire nations.

Chapter Twelve

THE MINI-EMPIRES

Below the first and second echelon warlords in our world lies a group of military empire builders upon which the United States could spend all of its do-good energies and monies if it seriously desired to play the role of world policeman. These warlords are attempting to build nuclear arsenals, stockpile missiles, produce poison gas, develop germ warfare capabilities, engage in terrorism, sponsor guerrilla movements, and perpetrate acts of terrorism in their petty pursuits of conquest.

Saddam Hussein took an additional step. This warlord of the mini-empire of Iraq boldly seized Kuwait. Overreaching their hand is a common mistake among warlords; they underestimate the resolve of free peoples. And since they do not tend to work well with other people, they assume that free folks won't go to the trouble of righting a wrong. The response of George Bush resulted in America's finest hour since World War II. Arguably, it was our finest international hour ever, since we simply did what we had to do in the two great world wars. Not so in Operation Desert Storm. We could have relied on negotiations only, which are an exercise in futility with a warlord, who reasons like this: what I now have is mine; what you have is negotiable. Or we could have taken unilateral action, forever incurring the wrath of many other nations, especially the Arab nations.

Amnesty International, a London-based human rights group, in its 1989 annual report, documented the slaughter of 5,000 Kurdish men, women, and children in a chemical warfare assault by Saddam in Halabja. At this writing, the United Nations continues to ferret out their weapons of mass destruction. And Saddam's warlord head is bloody, but unbowed.

Even space satellites have a dark side. The New York *Times*, in a front-page story on September 3, 1989, reported that non-superpowers are developing their own spy satellite systems . . .

A growing number of nations are building spy satellites or advocating such action, threatening to end the East-West monopoly on espionage from outer space.

Today only the United States, the Soviet Union and China have spy satellites that orbit hundreds of miles above the earth. Cameras in many of these craft take pictures of targets on the ground that are of military interest. Their pictures are either beamed to earth on encrypted radio signals or are returned in small capsules that plunge through the atmosphere and are later retrieved for processing. Other spy satellites gather electronic signals like military and civilian communications.

Experts say several nations are now taking steps to develop both photographic and electronic spy satellites, including Britain, France, Italy, Spain, Israel, and possibly India and South Africa. Some of these nations openly advertise their efforts. In other cases, experts have deduced the existence of secret military programs.

The proliferation of spy satellites could have a salutary effect of deterring surprise attacks, some experts say, or it could produce the opposite result, helping malevolent nations to plan and carry out an attack on hard-to-find targets. The spread of space surveillance technology is also expected to alter the diplomatic equation, freeing many nations from reliance on the current space powers for data.

Analysts say many nations are already using civilian "remote sensing" spacecraft as makeshift spy satellites. These craft routinely photograph the earth for scientific and commercial uses, like map making and forestry management. Although their images are far fuzzier than those of spy satellites, they offer some ability to view tanks, ships, missiles, aircraft, military sites and arms factories.

Sizable nations such as India and Pakistan are engaged in a small nuclear arms race. Libya and Iraq find poison gas to be most cost effective for their treasuries and within their technical reach. In poorer, hungrier nations such as Nicaragua and several African nations, traditional guerrilla insurgency without the benefit of higher technologies is the way of life. Millions suffer, nonetheless.

As through the ages, some of the most brutal conflicts are being waged between neighboring religions. Lebanon, for instance, suffers at the hands of Islamic Syria, a typical mini-empire nation.

Refugees are victims fleeing mini-empire conflicts. The United States Committee on Refugees reports this: the number of international refugees is increasing rapidly each year, with the 1988 total some 14.4 million persons. Most come from Afghanistan, Africa and Asia. Some are from Central America.

The July 3, 1989 issue of *Time* magazine reports the benevolent peoples of the world are suffering "compassion fatigue" as the funds available for operating refugee centers become scarcer, and as nations increasingly close their door to the settlement of new refugees.

A mild debate is being waged in the United States regarding the desirability of opening our borders to a million refugees and other immigrants annually. We assimilated this number early in the century, when we were rapidly growing in world stature. Some argue that the data show no serious negative effects; others fear for their jobs and are concerned that our social safety-net programs could be overloaded.

No mistake about it. The petty warlords and their mini-empires are a pesky problem. For our State Department, eternal vigilance must indeed be the price of freedom, as we quietly encourage self-determination and private enterprise in troubled spots where ambitious warlords are seeking domination. They often allow communists the opportunity to advance their cause and to earn cash from the sale of arms.

Since birds of a feather tend to flock together, there is always a possibility that these small-fry will band together to become a source of big trouble. More likely, they could become pawns of one of the major warlords.

The common people are powerless to resist the institutions formed by cruel leaders like Colonel Muammar al Qaddafi, Chief of State, Socialist People's Libyan Jamahiriya. In the era of Sun Tzu, when the world's population was only on the order of 100 million persons, Qaddafi would have rated top billing among the world's warlords. Today, he is merely an outstanding example of the type of persons who set up mini-empires.

Many aspire to join the Libyan colonel. Judging from the almost monthly attempt of a military coup somewhere in the world, there are, no doubt, dozens plotting against established governments at any given time.

In 1969 Colonel Qaddafi led a military revolution against the traditional monarchy. Western oil companies were at that time developing great reserves of crude oil in the Libyan desert. His timing was perfect: no sooner had he consolidated control than he had the opportunity to become a founder of OPEC. His mini-empire suddenly also became an oil empire! Libya took a rocket ride from a poverty-stricken agrarian nation to the country with the highest per-capita income in all of Africa.

Qaddafi used these new riches to launch a campaign exporting leftist and Islamic revolution all over the world. His revolutionary republic has worked especially hard to subvert governments in surrounding lands and toward the interior of Africa. Although the price of crude oil declined in the 1980s, moderating Qaddafi's maverick interventions, Libya still enjoys a per-capita income that is more than half the level in the United States. Enough money to produce lethal gas, a weapon almost as effective as an atomic bomb when delivered by urban guerrillas and released in a metropolitan center.

THE NORIEGA LESSON

Both Qaddafi and General Manuel Noriega of Panama made the same mistake. They overplayed their hands, provoking a quick military strike by the United States. We were successful in each instance. The Libyan troublemaker was put in his place; Noriega was put behind bars.

The world learned much about the inner workings of a man who establishes a mini-empire, when the private life of the Panamanian strong-man was disclosed. The Associated Press reported from Panama City, while Noriega was holed up in the Vatican embassy, that he was a warlock:

> Noriega practiced "santeria," which mixes African,
> Roman Catholic and American Indian deities and
> sometimes involves animal sacrifice.

> "That man is a devil," said a young woman in the poor
> neighborhood of El Chorrillo, a few blocks from the
> ruins of Noriega's Comandancia headquarters.

> "They better watch him. I don't want him to escape. He
> can turn himself into a boa or a dove and escape from
> the gringos," she said.

"We didn't want his dictatorship anymore because he was bringing in communism," said one woman. "Any Panamanian who did not agree with him, he would kick them out of their jobs and throw them in jail. He only had a bunch of thugs working for him."

Back to the tribal jungle. The mini-warlords place a great burden on our diplomatic and military people. We must constantly monitor their activities, document criminal conduct, and prepare numerous contingency plans in the event that we must, as with Libya, Panama, and Iraq, again take direct action.

A December 29, 1989 dispatch by Larry Jolidon of *USA Today* gave details of Noriega's rituals:

Army Chief Warrant Officer James Dibble easily has the oddest task of the U.S. invasion force here: he must sort out Manuel Noriega's religious practices.

Dibble, here from Fort Campbell, Ky., has sifted through the contents of the "ritual rooms" discovered in one of Noriega's luxury villas.

"I plan to prove that Noriega practiced ritual homicide," says Dibble, an occult expert.

Dibble says Noriega was "a demented man," a heavy drug user who had gone beyond manipulation to human sacrifice.

Noriega's basic method of influencing people, says Dibble, was to put personal documents, news clippings or handwritten lists of names in a bottle or under a stone, glob of wax or gelatin, or wrapped around a white candle.

"Having their names stuck in a pan or wrapped around a candle," Dibble says, "was Noriega's way of believing he controlled the people themselves."

The papers in Noriega's house bore the names of famous foreigners — George Bush, Ronald Reagan, Henry Kissinger, John Poindexter, Costa Rican President Oscar Arias — as well as many Panamanians, including new President Guillermo Endara.

> Noriega's patron saints, assigned by his "priestess," are St. George and St. Jude. Besides offering dried blood to appease them, says Dibble, Noriega wore red underwear "to ward off the evil eye."

While the military interdiction of Noriega's nefarious scheme was popular in this country and with the weary Panamanians, hemispheric opinion is another matter. We may have won the war but lost the hearts of Latin Americans. Our enemies are weaving a web of disinformation; they are saying that the gringos are waging a war against the poor nations and are supporting fascists who slaughter Roman Catholic clergy.

BUSINESS OPPORTUNITIES

Because of the often irrational and anti-American words and deeds of these strong men, business opportunities in the mini-empires should be approached with utmost caution, if at all.

Nations in this category offer some real challenges to would-be exporters of freedom. However, it must be remembered that, in spite of the fiercest of warlords and the harshest of institutions controlled by them, the yearning for freedom among the common people is almost uniform throughout the human race. We must, in most cases, be prepared to await the demise of the strong man presently in power, while concurrently building solid business, professional and trans-cultural relationships with the people.

Fortunately, we can look to Panama and see an elected official sitting as President. The Interglobalist will not make a commitment to a mini-empire predicated on the assumption that our marines or paratroopers will protect us. But it is comforting to know this: our government can still be provoked to employ gunboat diplomacy.

Yet few American businessmen become involved in an active mini-empire. Our people and our property become prime whipping-boys, then prized hostages. The real problem usually is this: many sound investments were made in Cuba, Iran, Lebanon, and the like, when the host government and the economy appeared to favor such action. Indeed; each of these three nations was regarded as an excellent risk ten to twenty years after World War II.

What to do then, since unexpected upheavals happen more often than the prudent business manager would like? The Interglobal Age manager hedges his bets by spreading his operations across as many national boundaries as possible — nothing new — our agrarian grandfathers were advised not to put all of their eggs in one basket.

Chapter Thirteen

THE ISLAMIC EMPIRES

Three of the world's greatest religious men espoused essentially the same philosophy as the golden rule. Gautama Buddha, for seven years, sought truth that could be applied to the suffering masses of India before he concluded that selfishness caused all the sorrow of the world. His plans for overcoming selfishness became Buddhism. About the same time, Confucius said, "What you do not like done to yourself, do not unto others."

Islam, on the other hand, teaches its disciples that *jihad* is not only honorable and fitting in advancing the will of Allah, but that death in a holy war is a quick route to heavenly rewards. Within a century or two, in the very cradle of Christianity, Islam conquered two-thirds of the world's Christians. Islam has proven to be the most effective enemy of Christianity. Communists, for all their propaganda and persecution, have not been able to approach this record established by Islam: Christians are either now extinct or a small, despised minority in Islamic lands where they once were a majority.

The domain of Islam is quite impressive: more than three-fourths of a billion people are nominal Moslems; hundreds of millions are devout, praying five times daily; tens of millions adhere strictly to all of the fundamentals of the faith; and millions daily have chanted, "Death to America!" Occasionally, such as in the bombing of the World Trade Center, they put these inflammatory words into action.

While Islam is often a destabilizing force, promoting its leaders' versions of the will of Allah through violence, the other major religions of the world usually tend to provide stability in a society by upholding the dignity of man and allowing freedom-seeking through peaceful means.

NATIONALISM VERSUS FUNDAMENTALISM

The great world wars of this century introduced the Islamic world to Western thought, resulting in two diametrically opposed approaches to the sociopolitical reconstruction of the Middle East: secular nationalism and Islamic fundamentalism. Religious and political differences and strong ambitions have further fragmented the Moslem world. There are many areas of agreement, however. All try to keep other religions from proselytizing Moslems. Almost all allow no democracy in the choice of their head of state. They are only slightly less united in their determination to eliminate the Jewish state in their midst.

This bad blood goes back to a sibling rivalry between Ishmael and Isaac, a rivalry foretold by an angel in *Genesis*:

> You shall name him Ishmael . . .

> He will be a wild donkey of a man . . . his hand will be against everyone . . . and he will live in hostility to the east of all his brothers.

ISLAM AND THE NORTHERN BEAR

The Soviet Union loved to fish in troubled waters. Since it was blocked from expansion toward the east by a Chinese Communist Party that prudently decided it wanted nothing to do with Soviet control, and on the west by a vigilant NATO defense system, the south provided the best long-term hope . . . with warm-water ports as a bonus. Fortunately, the Soviets made the typical warlord mistake; they overplayed their hand by attacking Afghanistan in order to demonstrate to the Islamic peoples within their own nation, and in the region, who really ruled the roost. They got a clear answer: Islam rules in its own territory.

With the demise of the Soviet Union, communist funding for Islamic warlords ground to a halt. Instead, neighboring Turkey and Iran began to compete for the favor of new, impoverished republics in Central Asia with such names as Kazakhstan, Uzbekistan, and Turkmenistan. As I write, the Turkish model of a secular Islamic state is favored by most of the new Islamic nations over the Iranian model, which features strict Islamic law ruling all facets of life in the country.

More importantly, rumors are flying concerning the transfer of weapons of mass destruction from the former Soviet stockpiles to Islamic warlords to their south. From the standpoint of these

Moslem warlords, don't bet against Ezekiel's war, discussed in a previous chapter, taking place in this decade.

ISLAM AND FREEDOM

Islam has been a serious barrier to the osmosis of freedom. Until recently, autocratic monarchs have worked hand-in-glove with the Moslem leaders. Secular encroachments within Islam have yet to produce much democracy and they have gained almost no freedom of religion. Indeed, freedom and human rights in the Islamic nations stretching from Mauritania to Malaysia leave much room for improvement, from women's rights in Iran to tolerance of the beliefs of others throughout the region. True democracies are scarce, too.

The glue unifying the global village is rational decisions based on facts and enlightened self-interest. And long-term self-interest lives and lets live. Increasingly, interglobal thinking finds common ground in our self-interest. But fervid religionists seeking to gain converts by force are obviously out of step. They are especially dangerous if they are eager to die while advancing their cause — by killing others.

Militant Islam could replace communism as the leading adversary of freedom and democracy.

BUSINESS OPPORTUNITIES

The business climate in the Moslem world ranges from private enterprise to Marxism. But even in markets that are ostensibly open, business must usually be done through established nationals. Those contemplating long-term projects in an Islamic empire should remember that fanatical fundamentalists are determined to repeat the "jihad" of 1979 in Iran and of 1989 in Beirut — in the Islamic country of your choice. Some Islamic nations are presently populated with fewer fanatics than Iran, but all are by nature volatile and easily incited. For instance, usually friendly Jordan sided with Saddam Hussein — overnight.

How radical was the change in Iran? One indication is the reception given President Dwight D. Eisenhower, who was so popular with the people of Tehran that they placed their expensive Persian carpets on the roadway from the airport to the palace of the Shah. His limousine travelled the entire journey only on carpets freely laid down by the common people! Today, Iran is probably the world's most fervently anti-American nation.

Egypt is a nation within the Islamic bloc that appears to have potential for cultivation by Americans with respect to increasing the freedom and democracy that already are in process. Cairo, with its ten million people, has a greater population than a number of the Moslem nations; it is the intellectual capital of Islam. Because of a high birth rate and limited arable land, Egypt has become highly dependent on foreign aid. Therefore, many developmental business enterprises and social programs are viable. Interglobalists, take note!

Americans interested in promoting freedom through food aid or agricultural development will find no shortage of opportunities in the Democratic Republic of Sudan, a nation with an annual per-capita income of about $400. Just naming a country a democratic republic does not make it so. Indeed, the leadership of these unfortunate peoples has made a mockery of the name by seeking to slaughter millions of Christians and animists.

Industrial development could be a more appropriate approach to the Republic of Turkey, whose constitution guarantees religious freedom. However, only a few thousand of the fifty million citizens would dare acknowledge public allegiance to any but Allah. Often, American business involvement could be a favorable factor in a gradual move toward more liberties in a nation that for hundreds of years controlled the region we now refer to as the Islamic Empire.

Prudent interglobal thinkers will tend to keep a very low profile: marketing through an Islamic distributor, or working through licensing agreements and joint ventures portraying the image of the Islamic partner.

Be wary in lands where *jihad* plus OPEC megabucks plus eager high-tech arms peddlers pose a real threat to interglobalism.

Chapter Fourteen

THE
NON-DEVELOPING
NATIONS

The destruction of the military and industrial might of the Japanese and European powers in World War II signaled the end of the colonial era. The colonies, often encouraged or led by communists, responded to this power vacuum with independence movements. The number of countries holding membership in the United Nations exploded during the next twenty years; some were Soviet puppets. Other new nations, while pro-Marxist, did not follow or totally embrace the communistic line. Unfortunately, most regimes were soon controlled by greedy warlords who perpetrated the worst of crimes by victimizing their own citizens through corruption. This violates one of warlord Sun's precepts: it is essential for the people to be fairly governed and happy with the administration in order to be successful as a nation and to wage war. Immediately after World War II, America concentrated most of its foreign policy attention and about twenty billion dollars of its cash on the Marshall Plan. We were immensely successful in helping devastated industrialized nations rebuild their economic systems.

FROM HOPE TO HOPELESS

Americans first began reaching out to what was called "the underdeveloped nations" with President Harry Truman's Point Four Program, administered by Dr. Henry G. Bennet, the internationally minded former president of the Oklahoma A&M College. As the cold war evolved and the sensitivities of the recipients of aid programs were considered, the common term for these newly independent and struggling nations was changed to the "Third

World." Thus, it was recognized that the three major groups of nations in the world in the 1950s and '60s were the Western industrialized nations, led by the United States; the Communist nations; and those non-industrialized nations who were struggling to better their lot.

Point Four soon became the Agency for International Development. Such institutions as the World Bank, the Export-Import Bank, and regional development banks came into being to help these new nations.

Since most were hungry, an agricultural development strategy, the green revolution, became a cornerstone of our aid efforts. Famine was indeed averted by this developmental scheme. Pessimism turned to optimism. The terminology for these young countries was changed to "the developing nations." Loan funds were made available based on increasingly optimistic assumptions. Events in most of these lands, however, did not follow a happy scenario. Energy prices escalated dramatically, as did interest rates. The industrialized countries experienced stagnation, then recession. For many of the most impoverished countries, the last two decades have proven to be nothing short of disaster. Most became non-developing nations.

The World Development Report for 1989, issued by the World Bank, states that many indebted African and Latin American nations remain trapped in economic stagnation and decline, despite recovery, growth, and prosperity in the industrialized countries. In 1988, these small debtor nations owed about a trillion dollars in total long-term debt outstanding to private and governmental lenders. In inflation-adjusted terms, the average person in these indebted countries is now about seven percent poorer than in 1980.

Since September, 1985, the fifteen most-indebted nations only received three billion dollars in new loans from commercial banks, while they paid more than twenty billion dollars in interest, according to Morgan Guaranty Trust Company of New York. In response to this situation, President Bush announced in July, 1989, the decision to forgive one billion dollars in debt owed to this government by sixteen of the poorest African nations.

In the Western Hemisphere, the debt problem carries a bigger price tag than with the African nations, and the economic cancer extends all the way from Tijuana to Tierra del Fuego. Latin America is falling apart. There is a massive deterioration of the region's infrastructure. Just to repair the roads could cost six billion dollars, more than twice the sum of foreign aid infused into the region last year.

The Economist, June 24, 1989, reports that creditors sapped a net of twenty-four billion dollars out of Latin America in 1988. This number is arrived at by adding interest and principal payments and deducting new loans. The magazine further reports that capital flight has been a great problem for the Latin American nations, with some four hundred billion dollars of privately owned capital having been removed from banks in the region and deposited in North America and Europe in recent years. They estimate that Mexico leads the way with eighty billion dollars, followed by Venezuela with sixty billion; Argentina with fifty billion; and Brazil with some forty billion dollars. If the citizens had confidence in their government and their business climate, these funds would be invested locally and would be working in the development of their nations, which have considerable human and raw material resources.

Argentina, once ranked with Spain in its degree of development, has gone through an economic free-fall. Its two nuclear power plants were closed for lack of spare parts. Social unrest that has produced food riots and looting has not gone away.

Perhaps the worst sign described by the World Bank report was that many of the financial institutions in these non-developing nations are now "insolvent on an unprecedented scale."

It matters little to the desperate citizens of these nations, many of whom have resorted to shoplifting, looting, and robbery in order to survive, that the communist economic system has failed in its heartland. All they know is that the system they have is not working and they desperately need anything that offers hope. Troubled waters, indeed!

Unfortunately, the oppressed people of the debt-ridden, non-developing nations are unable to see that Nicaragua, once a prosperous Central American nation, is now wreaked with a runaway inflation and has become one of the poorest nations in the Western Hemisphere, under the tutelage of the Soviets and Cuba. Daniel Ortega, with considerable economic and military assistance from the communist allies, seems to have done the almost impossible: bankrupted a close neighbor of the United States . . . a small price, he and his communist cohorts no doubt feel, for having poked a finger in the eye of Uncle Sam and having briefly established a North American beachhead for Soviet communism.

Nicaragua and Cuba are Western Hemisphere examples of the universal failure of the communist economic system. The capitalist, socialistic, and mixed economic systems of the Western world have produced mixed economic results in the post-World War II era, primarily depending upon governmental management as well as the experience the people of the nation have had in commerce and industry; communism as an economic model has utterly failed everywhere.

Most of these non-developing nations have at least attempted to establish a democratic form of government — at one time or another. Inexperience, graft, and incompetence have been the principal reasons for the failure of fledgling democracies. In some cases, elected officials were overthrown by communist or military coups even though they were performing reasonably well.

The issue is clear: non-development provides the enemies of freedom with the unrest they need to destroy four decades of painful progress in dozens of nations. Some analysts say the Cold War pitted East against West. It now appears that the rich in the north get richer, while the poor in the south get poorer . . . clearly, an unhealthy situation.

BUSINESS OPPORTUNITIES

A business newsletter is saying Brazil's time has arrived, but the same statement was commonly made three decades ago. The country has such potential: sixth largest population in the world; tenth largest economy; second only to the United States in agricultural exports; vast agricultural potential; an industrial base from which to build. It seemed that Brazil's technocratic government had it well on the way to becoming a commercial empire in the 1970s. But this important nation has never recovered from the shock of the OPEC oil price increase. And it is being crushed by an excessive debt service burden. Inflation, which was rampant in the 1960s, then brought under control in the 1970s, is raging again. Brazil reestablished democracy at the national level as it began the '90s, only to impeach the president in 1992.

Interglobal managers can learn to live with inflation. The newsletter editor may have a point: Brazil deserves a serious look-see. One enterprising American group has accumulated two million acres of undeveloped land in the *campo cerrado*. The government recently completed a paved highway linking their land to the port city of Salvador and the capital city of Brasilia. They believe their twenty years of research has developed farming techniques that will make them world-class competitors in the production of rice, soybeans, beef, pork, poultry, oranges, and cashews. They count on their diversity of products as a hedge against the cyclical nature of agricultural commodity markets.

Argentina and Mexico are other debt-ridden nations with potential for profit . . . given interglobal prudence. Because of recent changes, Mexico is discussed as a labor empire. Among the African countries, the development of export enterprises appears to hold the best promise. The fertile soils of East Africa easily produce an abundance of crops, yet in several nations the per-hectare yields are little better than in colonial times. Mineral production and processing hold promise in other countries south of the Sahara.

Marxist revolution or neo-communism could unexpectedly engulf a business enterprise almost anywhere in the non-developing empire. Yet, if we sit on our hands, such groups, along with right-wing military dictatorships, are more likely to topple today's fragile leadership.

So, interglobal strategy calls for a proactive approach; count the cost and start a developmental export-oriented business. Hire people, who in turn become consumers; help a non-performer move up into the labor empire. The annual population growth rate is almost twice the 1.7% world average, so they desperately need jobs: jobs that will for the most part be generated only by hardy, creative interglobalists from the Industrialized Empire nations.

Chapter Fifteen

THE OUTCASTS

I srael and South Africa seem to stand alone in the community of nations: friendless and subject almost daily to attack by the media and the United Nations. But how much more oppressive are their regimes than those of many of the warlords we have considered? Both have a form of democracy and are making an honest effort to improve the lot of their dissidents. Are they the cruelest of empires and warlords, or victims of a Big Lie media campaign? Are they being set up by a master warlord's plot? What would the Russians gain from a two-step southern adventure? Could a smiling master politician from the northland convince the world that he was simply spanking the neighborhood bad boys by marching on one or both of them?

ISRAEL

The Israeli decision, in July 1989, to place conditions upon the American peace overture that are totally unacceptable to Israel's adversaries signals a siege mentality that invites opportunism.

By 1992 this American insistence on Israel giving up land for peace with its Arab neighbors had thrown an election to the Labor Party, which now has favor with our State Department and has our guarantee on a ten billion dollar loan. Meanwhile, negotiations for peace in the Middle East seem to show little progress.

Concurrently, Russia seems to be drifting closer to neo-communism. And what could unify their bedraggled citizens quicker and tighter than the prospect of a war of hate against Israel, where some 600,000 former Soviets have already fled? It worked for Hitler!

While the Russians could not logically expect all the Islamic Middle Eastern nations to join in an alliance, even with the guarantee of a destruction of their hated enemy, they should be able to preside over a cartelization of world oil that could seriously impair the capabilities of other nations to conduct a protracted war. Additionally, they would gain access to great mineral reserves, including fertilizers needed in the U.S.S.R., warm-water ports for their fleets, and control of the Suez Canal.

"The expert commander strikes only when the situation assures victory," was a favorite Sun precept. Except in the case of Afghanistan, the Soviet warlords have very conservatively followed this teaching. Some combination of three factors could lure the Russians to attack Israel: the belief that neither Europe nor America would fire ICBM's or come to the aid of Israel, desperation to retain power in their own motherland and thus feeling forced to violate Sun's cardinal principle, or the need to come to the aid of one or more of their client nations being defeated by Israel.

BEYOND ISRAEL

But let's suppose that a new warlord in Moscow is not only world-class, let's suppose he is all-time world-class. We have already seen that international communism holds all the all-time records for warlords. There is a strong conspiracy theory afoot, discounted by most as being the figment of the imagination of Cold War hawks who refuse to give up the fight. This theory states: the communist masters saw that they could not win the way they were going, so they killed off Soviet communism, only to resurrect it in a few years as neo-communism, with the same old goal of world conquest.

Whether this theory holds any water or not is immaterial. Warlords with the same old goals persist. And, more importantly, so do the weapons for achieving this conquest.

So, if mother Russia is to come out of her present hibernation with fangs bared and claws swinging, why stop with Israel when the second largest continent lies undefended just beyond?

SOUTH AFRICA

President Bush called it the Revolution of '89. But as he coined this phrase speaking to the Congress and the nation, the Interglobal Revolution continued to startle the world with the unexpected event in the unexpected place — President F.W. de Klerk met many of the blacks' demands and released Nelson Mandela!

Prime Minister Margaret Thatcher of Britain responded by lifting sanctions. Many Americans said the sanctions had worked, but awaited more progress. Trinity Broadcasting Network, with stations in the United States and South Africa, saw the hand of

God working through leaders on both sides who had recently been born again.

But the pattern was clear: unexpected, dramatic change for the better!

Perhaps de Klerk and Mandela can negotiate a settlement both sides will abide by. It will, however, be a modern miracle.

If there is no miracle, and the Soviets still venture southward in either a greedy or a desperate grab of Israel and the Suez, it would be a much easier step to move on to the conquest of South Africa since Marxist governments already exist along the way in Ethiopia, Madagaskar, and Mozambique. Just as a "police action" would be very popular among Israel's Arab neighbors, the black neighbors of South Africa would, for the most part, be eager to join in claiming the spoils of a conquest of the practitioners of apartheid.

Alternatively, it is well within Russian capability to move first against South Africa, should this target of opportunity appear to be a better option than Israel. East African nations along the way should be no more able to defend themselves than were the Ethiopians able to resist the Italian invasion just before World War II.

The lush savannahs of East Africa's wild kingdom should assure the Soviets of a reliable source of food for their peoples, while South Africa would provide them a monopoly in some strategic minerals used in aircraft, aerospace, and other high-technology industries. The diamonds and the gold would be a fringe benefit. Thus, in two steps, the Soviets could assure themselves of enough control of both petroleum and strategic minerals to effectively prevent any prospective enemy from waging a protracted war against them. A Soviet presence in South Africa, along with a popular move to abolish the existing white rule in that nation, could be expected by the Soviets to yield immense dividends in terms of troubled African nations turning to a neo-communistic government. The strategic value of control of both the Suez Canal and the Cape of Good Hope would be difficult to overestimate.

Warlord Sun is one of the few great military analysts who has taken into proper consideration the financial and human expenses of warfare. He preferred never to bloody a sword . . . ruin by subversion was his motto.

His next option was to strike swiftly and decisively with a fatal blow to the enemy. A protracted war or siege was something to be considered only as a last resort. Both of these moves by the U.S.S.R. would be very acceptable risks to Sun.

112

In fact, the net drain on the aggressor forces would be projected to be minimal in the short term and the benefits to be highly positive in the medium to long term.

A conservative approach to South Africa would be to win from within, without deploying troops. An intermediate strategy would be for the Soviets to attack after having absorbed one or more additional neighboring nations through subversion . . . then attack through this land base. Another low-cost strategy would be to detonate nuclear devices in the white population centers.

Beginning in February 1990, moves by the South African government toward providing human rights for the black majority in South Africa could possibly even play into the hands of the sophisticated neo-communists. Fighting could break out between militant blacks, demanding immediate, complete freedom, desegregation, and democracy, and right-wing whites trying to protect their turf. Troubled waters such as these could give the Russians the opportunity to rally the black neighborhood and move in to establish order — all without so much as a slap on the wrist by the United Nations, if they are both adroit and lucky.

South African strategic planners, of course, thought through such a worst-case scenario. On March 24, 1993, President de Klerk made a dramatic confession: his nation in 1989 had constructed several atomic bombs. However, they were never tested and were subsequently dismantled. Thus, South Africa continues to seek to distance itself from our outcast empire category.

SUMMARY

Western proponents of rising to Israel's or South Africa's defense would have a difficult time inspiring people of the "me" generation to fight a battle on a distant field with the risk of the almost certain annihilation of their homeland and families. A nuclear strike by America would invite the instant annihilation of our civilization.

STAR WARS

Although the United States proclaimed a new era in space when, in November 1992, we launched the first Star Wars hardware, we are a long way from being able to protect our nation from all of the many warheads now poised and ready to be launched against us from Russia. Until the day arrives that we can indeed interdict almost all of them, we remain quite vulnerable to nuclear blackmail. As a practical matter, in the instance under consideration, we likely would never lift a nuke as we tried

113

to talk the new Russian warlord out of gobbling up Israel, South Africa, and points in between.

Resistance with conventional forces would likewise be deemed too costly and too unlikely to succeed. What we would fail to take into account is this: success in Africa by neo-communists probably would lead to successes in Latin America, home of the other half of the non-developing nations. Thus, the warlord-chessmaster would anticipate a final confrontation in world conquest along the Rio Grande . . . with or without the nuclear exchange, since as a truly global warlord, the citizens left behind in the Russian homeland would be considered expendable. If so, he would win Warlord Sun's "Man of the Century" award!

For their part, the two outcasts have formed an ad-hoc mutual protection society. Each is helping the other in the development of a complete system of modern weapons, including the atomic bomb, missiles, and combat aircraft. Judging by the budget and manpower dedicated to this armament program, each must believe that their nation is in imminent danger of attack by a very strong foe.

Israel, the more aggressive of the two, also has an excellent intelligence apparatus and has been known to make preemptive strikes. Such a nuclear first strike could bring down the pre-planned wrath of the Russian neo-communists . . . with the blessings of most of the rest of the world.

The status of the dissidents in Israel and South Africa is perhaps only about the world average with regard to quality of life and freedom. Much improvement is needed. However, there is an alternative that could be much worse. They could be pawns, inviting a conquest that would not be blocked by the West — except with words, which break no neo-communist bones.

BUSINESS OPTIONS

Considerable pressure is being exerted on the American business community to make "ethical investments." This is left-wing shorthand for precluding doing any business in South Africa, not for disinvesting in companies that sponsor violent movies and television programs or that produce and distribute pornographic materials.

Thus, a project of any size in South Africa could subject a company and its personnel to criticism as well as a boycott of both its investment securities and its products at home.

For a single issue on which progress is being made, a nation that produces twenty-five percent of the gross national product of sub-Saharan (black) Africa and is the world's biggest exporter of non-petroleum minerals is to be hung out to be picked to pieces by whatever warlord comes along!

A Russian chessmaster could be such a warlord. The two nations dominate world gold and strategic mineral production. If the now-delicate world economy could be panicked into a simple stampede away from paper money and toward hard assets, control of South Africa could be invaluable to the Russian bear. A gold-backed ruble could quickly move to the forefront in world currency markets, which are approaching the trillion-dollars-per-day level of transfers.

Boycott South Africa? "Let him who is without sin cast the first stone." This two thousand year old comment to a lynch mob is good interglobal advice for a nation that slaughters a million unborn babies a year and exports movies extolling every form of vice known to man and demon . . . except racial prejudice.

What then of Israel? A nation that has technology and the availability of capital, but will have increasing problems with exports. Dare we use the word anti-Semitism? As the United States and Israel feel increasing pressures to assimilate Jews from the former Soviet Union into already beleaguered economies, such a movement may arise. More likely, one of the alternative scenarios that would cause a serious decline in living standards in the United States would be the factor to precipitate anti-Semitism. Rich Jews are a convenient whipping boy in times of economic distress; the germ of an alleged master conspiracy by Jewish peoples is ever-present. A strong world bias against Jewish people could result in a reactionary conversion of currencies to hard assets and a new wave of migration to the safe haven of the State of Israel. Such an influx of wealth by the world's rich, talented Jews would attract the attention of a major warlord; a neo-communist, for instance. It is the influx of poor Russian Jews — and the possibility of the exodus of rich Jews from the West — that create the best business opportunities for interglobal entrepreneurs in these outcast empires.

Chapter Sixteen

THE GLOBAL VILLAGE

A comparison of three post-World War II growth rates tells us that the world has been transformed into a global village at a rapid rate. During the past forty years, the world's population has doubled. Economic growth was two and one-half times faster than the population growth; thus, the average citizen on the planet was favored with a 250% increase in real income. An impressive accomplishment — yet world trade grew as fast as the world economy!

And we have become a Global Village. Some of the characteristics of the village are listed below.

TRANSPORTATION AND DISTRIBUTION

In order for least-cost sourcing of manufactured goods to work on a global scale, the cost of transportation to a port, shipping across the ocean, unloading, transportation to a distribution center, and final shipment to the dealer had to become more than competitive with manufacturing within an industrialized nation such as the United States — in some cases, even when a modest tariff is paid to gain access to the market. Hats off to an efficient system!

COMMUNICATIONS

The telex, the telephone, and the fax have shrunk instant communication across the world to the size of the village square on market day.

LANGUAGE

Common trade languages have been adopted as a matter of practicality for thousands of years. For instance, Greek remained the standard second language for commerce throughout the Roman Empire for hundreds of years after the Greek Empire fell.

Fortunately for Americans, English-speaking nations have dominated international business for most of the last three hundred years. Only in a few backwater former French colonies — Chad, for instance — does the English-speaking business person experience serious difficulties in conducting business in his native tongue, an advantage we too often take for granted.

EDUCATION

Again, Americans are blessed. Our business and technical graduates from abroad are now leaders in their nations. Now most enjoy visiting with us about how things are here. Many others come here for conventions, seminars and workshops. We educate the world. Unfortunately, some use illegal and unethical means to gain trade secrets that have cost us millions of dollars; intellectual property protection is a growing issue in our village.

TRADE WARS

The role of government is changing rapidly. No longer is the main concern to protect citizens from the barbarians (to use the classical Chinese concept) on the outside; the concern is to seek free and equitable access to markets in the village. Trade, by definition, is a two-way street; we cannot forever purchase the wonderful Japanese toys, watches, electronic appliances, and autos without selling them something in return. Really!

Life was less complicated a few thousand years ago and everyone then understood this principle. You had to give up something of yours in order to barter for something that you wanted more but that belonged to someone else. Look for barter to make a comeback in the village; a number of nations in the marketplace are running out of hard currencies.

Counterpurchase is sophisticated barter. As the communist and formerly communist nations have sought to do business with Americans, the sale of our products is normally tied to the purchase of a similar dollar amount of something they would like to export. We may as well get used to this complication if we wish to be a world heavyweight exporter. With our deficit, we cannot afford to take only the easier cash sales.

Offsets are really complicated. The vendor undertakes to compensate the country buying the American product for the loss of local technology development, currency, jobs and whatever intangibles they can negotiate. What would happen if the United States had demanded such arrangements before we lost our smokestacks?

Many nations insist that certain industries may be penetrated by outsiders only through co-production. Fortunately, this is relatively simple; an agreement is reached in which the product is manufactured within the host nation.

Why bother with all these complicated mechanisms, the typical American asks; all we want to do is make a sale and spend the money. To balance our national trading is one reason. Another is that countertrade is a sort of guerrilla warfare that stops short of the tariff wars demanded by special interest groups in almost all nations.

We must choose a cold war — countertrade, rather than a hot war of tit-for-tat tariff battles in the Interglobal Age!

Many contrarians like to forecast that economic chaos is around the corner and that hard assets such as gold, silver, and diamonds will be preferred to even the soundest of today's currencies. Contrarians have always been around; they buy stock in a company when most analysts are advising their clients to sell it. Some see the second stage as being a cashless global village with a universal debit card — and implanting the magnetic strip in the skin on the back of the hand would be a convenient way of making sure you never leave home without it.

The disadvantage of the debit card is that some warlord might be able to control everything, in one big computer. So, perhaps a free market barter system could evolve, with refinements.

Could the village marketplace indeed go full cycle?

INTERDEPENDENCE

Hopefully not. We must talk and act in long-term, interdependent ways. Short-term thinking will invariably lead to trade wars. Patience may be the cardinal virtue of the Interglobal Age; patience by the individual rapees of the communist conquest of the Russian Empire, China, Eastern Europe, and a score of other nations who feel that, even after the Interglobal Revolution, theirs is a lost generation, given over to recovery; patience by the Israelis and the Palestinians who seek a peaceful, moderate solution to their conflict; patience by the black majority and the whites who developed South Africa's abundant resources; and patience and cooperation by nations seeking to rectify trade imbalances.

In *Winning the Countertrade War*, Matt Schaffer suggests creative countertrade solutions to trade imbalances as an alternative to seemingly inevitable trade wars. But these require patience not presently seen in most American boardrooms and executive suites.

LEADERSHIP AND STATESMANSHIP

Ralph H. Kilmann, Teresa Joyce Covin, and associates in *Corporate Transformation* argue that organizations are man's greatest invention. They therefore see the revitalizing of our corporate structures as the great need for the '90s, even though more than half of the companies on the "Fortune" list of the 1,000 largest U.S. corporations have undergone significant reorganization recently. These authors do, however, almost as an afterthought, note the need for and the difficulty of changing personal attitudes at all levels in American corporations.

The philosophy of this book is the reverse: change to interglobal thinking, from top to bottom, and rectifying organizational inefficiencies, will come almost, but not quite, as a natural result.

The Interglobal Age. A time when the patient prosper. A time that tries men's souls in such a way that the true leaders and statesmen rise to the helm of our great business and governmental organizations.

We have tried them all: the engineer of the '50s when production was needed to fill pent-up demand; the accountant when the numbers got messed up; the MBA when the bean-counters faltered; the salesman when competition became fierce. Make way for the patient, balanced leader: the corporate statesman. The interglobalist.

VILLAGE PHILOSOPHY

As the corporate statesman begins rising to the prominence formerly reserved for Secretaries of State and Chairmen of the Joint Chiefs of Staff, intellectuals, historians, and philosophers will go to work explaining what all this means in terms they understand. It has always been so.

Georg Wilhelm Friedrich Hegel developed a theory that history is a process with a beginning and an end. Karl Marx taught that this culmination of economic and political history would be an unending communist utopia. History was proving him wrong: dead wrong.

Francis Fukuyama was acclaimed an intellectual hero by American conservatives in 1989 when he proclaimed a different end to historic evolution: responsible capitalism with a democratic government.

Will our world indeed move to what disciples of Hegel have termed an homogenous state — stamped from the American mold? Not if the warlords, both in government and in business, can help it.

Responsible capitalism with democratic government is the essence of interglobalism. In spite of all the obstacles that the most depraved of men can and will throw up, it is the pattern for life in the global village.

Fukuyama and Chee are two Asian-Americans who have seen the future. The interglobal village that lies beyond the Interglobal Revolution!

PART FOUR

The Forward Look

Chapter Seventeen

COMMON WISDOM

Before the time of Warlord Sun, battle planning was primarily a spiritual affair. The two sides encamped opposite each other for a few days while the seers studied tea leaves, stars, and other methods of divination, and while the commanders made blood sacrifices. The appropriate moment for joining battle was selected by the mystics, who normally confidently predicted victory for their leader.

Sun introduced the Age of Reason to the art of planning. The Age of Reason came to Europe almost two thousand years later. It prevailed in the United States until recently, when the musical *Hair* appeared on Broadway:

> The moon is in the seventh house, and Jupiter aligns
> with Mars, Then peace will guide the planets and love
> will steer the stars.

Thus, the New Age movement has revived ancient mystical astrology, asserting that we are entering the seventh millennium, the Age of Aquarius, a time of peace and tranquility. And their stargazing concurs with common wisdom. Coincidence?

Most planners today still prefer to take the inward look, the outward look, then make projections into the future. With computer graphics, three projections are often made, each in a different color. The middle, most likely scenario, is compared with a more optimistic and a more pessimistic projection on either side. Unfortunately, time and chance frequently cause the outcome to be as far from the projection as the ancient Chinese and Chaldean spiritists' predictions were from their outcomes.

For instance, Exxon is reported to have declined to enter an oil shale project in the late 1960s because they projected the price of crude oil at a three-dollars-per-barrel level, a price that would not justify the expense of extracting oil from the shale. Instead, OPEC less than a decade later caused artificial shortages to increase market prices to over thirty dollars per barrel — ten times the level projected by Exxon's finest minds!

But the story does not end there. Exxon planners fell next into the ditch on the other side of the road! A new management became acclimated to the OPEC price environment and invested heavily in Colorado oil shale. OPEC, fearing alternate sources of energy, increased production and let prices fall to as low as ten dollars per barrel. Exxon shelved the mammoth shale project.

Therefore, in view of the high risk in prognosticating, even by the largest and best-informed organizations, common wisdom will be compared with views of selected contrarians. The reader may then select his favorite — or write his own.

Assumptions are the stuff projections are made of. Most projections simply extrapolate the trends of the past into the future with some degree of fine-tuning upward or downward depending on the information on which the assumptions are based. Graphic presentations usually present the historic trend as a line with one, two, or three projections that do not deviate dramatically from the trend. Conservatism is the order of the day, so planners rarely predict such fundamental changes as the OPEC cartel or the Interglobal Revolution.

AFTER THE COLD WAR

Common wisdom says that the Revolution of '89 signalled the end of the cold war. We won! At this writing, however, the massive hardliner majority in the Russian parliament is sending us this message: the odds are about even that the cold war will be rekindled.

Another major tenet prevails today: we have learned to tinker with the world economic system so that major cycles of inflation and depression have largely become a thing of the past. Leaders of the industrial powers meet each year at the economic summit to keep everything under control. This tells us that the global village has arrived and that business, not war, is the business most discussed by the village elders.

But world leaders are aware that the poorest and most heavily indebted nations need their help. So the big business of the 1989 economic summit in Paris was for the members to convince each other that they would contribute their fair share to this global charity. The global village concept has now filtered down to the state house. Atlanta's mayor, Andrew Young, in addressing a recent Governors' Conference, exhorted the assembled executives to gird their states for worldwide economic competition.

123

George Will, in an August 14, 1989 *Newsweek* editorial, professed boredom with the contemplation of moving from the cold war conflict to a "bourgeois civil society . . . a commercial world. Evil brought out the best in the West. What now that the West has won?" Perhaps Will worries about this: without a global antagonist, Americans will have less need for the news media.

One of the biggest mistakes made by business planners is their failure to take into account that competitive planners are also looking at the same markets and making similar assumptions, which will be acted on by management in a similar manner. The result: excessive production capacity in an industry; empty office space; unsold merchandise. A number of nations are planning to get at least their share of the prosperity pie in the Interglobal Age. Unification means clout for the Europeans. Hard work, education, and central planning is the Chinese formula, but they and the former Soviets, the labor empires, and the non-developing nations all have a long way to go before they are invited to the economic summit, which is presently restricted to an elite seven most-industrialized nations.

While many outsiders see the United States and Japan joining Britain as declining empires, the citizens of these prosperous nations prefer to look only at today, rather than endure the discipline of a fearless look forward. The optimistic projection shows America making a comeback with new technologies, global entrepreneurial nichemanship, or a grand cooperation between government, business and labor (the Japanese model); it will be America's golden age, they say.

The optimists talk of advances in basic sciences, computers, medicine, and human nutrition. Academicians William Baumol, Sue Anne Batey Blackman, and Edward Wolff, in *Productivity and American Leadership*, point with pride to our world leadership in output per worker: $41,362 in 1988, compared with $33,489 in Germany and only $29,375 in Japan.

Unfortunately, the name of the game is unit cost, not productivity. Market demand and quality are other factors. American automobile makers are finally closing the quality gap on the Japanese.

Popular newspaper columnists are debating: should the United States mount a freedom/democracy campaign, or should we simply let osmosis run its course? Heads we win; tails we win. Or so says common wisdom.

Businessmen of the world are not debating. They are trying to find hotel rooms in off-the-beaten-path empires. America must compete. With interglobal thinking and action, we can more than compete: we can redefine international business. The new definition is Interglobal Age business.

124

Chapter Eighteen

THE CONTRARIANS SPEAK

H istory seems to teach us that it is unlikely that everything will go quite so well as common wisdom indicates. On the 50th anniversary of Hitler launching World War II, a Media General-Associated Press poll found that sixty percent of Americans expected World War III within two decades. Should such a war break out, fifty-four percent of those polled said it would escalate into an all-out nuclear war. Most thought a holocaust could happen!

Thus, our common people may not fully share the optimism of the intellectuals, the writers, and the planners.

Meanwhile, localized skirmishes continue to proliferate. In the perceived power vacuum, the one hundred ninety-two non-aligned nations, in their most recent meeting, no longer launched diatribes against "imperialists." Their troubles are more often internal, or with the nation next door. Economic development, freedom for their people, and regional tranquility are emerging as the issues for these maturing nations, which are mostly now thirtysomething years old.

One or more of the following scenarios may have a highly significant impact on the cause of freedom, business, and government before the beginning of the third millennium A.D. Unfortunately, planning is not an exact science — it is only an art; we cannot now say which ones will come to pass, if any.

BURSTING BUBBLES

One of the most disquieting of the projections made by contrarians is that economic bubbles will burst in the United States, resulting in a muddle-down of our economy and possibly of the world economy. Outsiders seem highly concerned, while insiders are willing to debate that the bubbles even exist.

Our bubbles include the chronic governmental deficits, our mountainous trade deficits, and the bad debts on the books of our banks.

HIGH-TECH TERRORISM

Islamic fundamentalists have warned that they are ready to launch an attack that will "shock everyone." It would be shocking indeed if a small, nondescript freighter fired a surface-to-air missile with a nuclear or poison gas warhead at point-blank range into the midst of London, Washington, or New York, simply as an instrument of radical anti-Western policy. Forget the missile. A low-tech suicide squad could do the same job very well. Today's terrorists, including the drug lords, have extremely deep pockets, everything to gain, and so little to lose. Would the world economic system panic? Was the van-bombing of the World Trade Center just a low-tech opening shot?

MONEY FLIGHT

A scenario worse than the 1929 fiasco could be imagined if the bubbles burst or if high-tech terrorists struck. Currencies would seek hard assets — gold, silver, and the like.

ULTRANATIONALISM

Strong nationalism, even fascism, may be expected from somewhere in the world before the Interglobal Age is very mature — hopefully, only in a mini-empire or two.

The transition from nationalism to the Interglobal Age will be difficult for many leaders and their nations. Should the leader be strong and endued with the charisma of a Kennedy, and should the nation also be powerful — World War III could result!

FAMINE

In a world that is growing at ninety million persons per year, that lacks an effective grain reserve, and that is faced with a rapidly deteriorating environment, the specter of famine must be considered.

Natural disasters have already taken a toll on our normal food reserves. In 1987 Asia was hit both with floods and drought, and world rice prices soared. The rice reserve has never recovered.

The 1988 drought in the center of the North American continent briefly more than doubled soybean prices. This price rationing alone kept the world from running out of soybeans and soybean oil meal. But livestock production was limited, protein for human nutrition was lacking, and malnutrition increased in the poor nations.

Production must increase or famine will greet us in the 1990s. There is no option. We are only one crop failure away from world famine.

Yet the problems continue to multiply. In addition to the global warming trend, volcanic clouds are causing agronomists to worry that such clouds could easily reduce the amount of sunlight available to growing crops, resulting in potentially critical reductions in yields.

But why should the rich, self-centered, industrialized nations concern themselves with famine? We can simply turn off the television set when it shows us the starving Africans. Here's why: food price increases come at the expense of the consumption of industrial products. Economic disruption then ensues.

SOCIAL DISORDER

Any of the preceding events could provoke social disorder unprecedented on this globe and make it very difficult for governments to establish a stable basis for economic reconstruction.

Of all generations in history, the spoiled-rotten "Me" generation believes that society owes it a living — a luxurious living by the standard of any other age. Would they not demand such rights? And if the government should not be able to provide for their expectations, would they not go to the streets? Would they, then, not steal and loot to satisfy their desires? Mobs sacked a portion of Los Angeles in 1992 with less provocation.

NEO-COMMUNIST ADVENTURE

Suppose Russia opts for a bold — or desperate — thrust southward to Israel and the Suez Canal, to South Africa and the Cape of Good Hope. They could then interdict shipping, strategic minerals and petroleum, thus creating a choking effect that could bring the commercial empires to heel.

However, not a shred of evidence can be found that a single soul believes there is a reasonable chance that a new Russian warlord would dare perpetrate so dastardly a deed. At least not a soul in our media.

Not so in the last days of Soviet Union. David Remnick, writing for the Washington *Post* from Leningrad, reported:

> . . . one recent night, however, a group of about one hundred evangelical Baptists gathered on the steps to play guitars and sing hymns . . . in between songs, their leader read aloud from the *Book of Revelation.*

Revelation? Evangelicals bent on winning converts here have long enjoyed the freedom of using public gathering places as a forum. But the *Book of Revelation* is normally reserved for the faithful. Many of them affirm that this futuristic last book of the Bible tells them that the born-again may be whisked away to heavenly rewards at any moment, leaving the unbelievers to cope as best they can with the cataclysmic events that follow. There is some disagreement as to whether this "rapture" takes place just before or after the assault by the Russians, Iran, Ethiopia, Libya and other allies, which is foretold by the prophet Ezekiel.

An untutored Russian pastor is fortunate if his library extends beyond a Bible, while his Western counterpart has a postgraduate-level seminary degree, complete with his denomination's version of systematic theology. What could they possibly know about the future of their troubled country?

NUCLEAR WINTER

Suppose the neo-communists succumb to the temptation to head south. And suppose they miscalculate; suppose the United States bites the bullet and fires a few nuclear warning shots. No list of doomsday possibilities would be complete without the unthinkable: millions of deaths in the metropolitan centers; radiation sickness and death; and perhaps an even greater number of deaths across the Northern Hemisphere from starvation during a years-long nuclear winter. Just when we thought the danger was past. Remember this: the fallout from just one volcanic eruption seriously moderated our weather in the summer of 1992!

MINI-EMPIRE AGGRESSION

More likely, the arms race has shifted to the mini-empires. The old-fashioned atomic bomb, biological agents, or World War I vintage poison gas could be the weapon of choice to supplement or replace guerrilla activity.

We postulate that these incidents will be mostly localized conflicts. However, they could be directed against the United States. This serious scenario could become a cause for grave concern in the unlikely event the semi-civilized leaders of the drug and mini-empires begin acting in concert.

PLAGUE

The world's population grew very slowly before Louis Pasteur discovered that microscopic organisms cause disease. About one billion people were alive in 1849 when Pasteur was appointed professor on the Faculty of Science in Strasbourg. The world's population increased by fifty percent during his tenure there and at the Pasteur Institute. Pasteurization, vaccination, and sanitation resulted in the addition of another one billion persons by the onset of World War II.

This cruel war cost fifty million lives, two-thirds civilian, but it only slowed population growth. Development of antibiotics during that war removed the last major barrier to population explosion. The five billion milestone was reached in the late 1980s. Thus, the world's population has increased five-fold in less than one hundred and fifty years; disease, not war, has ever been man's mortal foe.

AIDS is now epidemic in the United States; it is approaching plague proportions in Central Africa. Conventional wisdom says a cure will be found. If not, plague is at the door.

Rapidly increasing health care costs, like food-price escalations, occur at the expense of expenditures in manufactured goods. The world economy can't afford a plague.

NATURAL CATACLYSM

The year 1989: hurricane and earthquake. Some were reminded that our complex society could conceivably be torn asunder by sudden, unexpected natural forces. Scientists say the global warming trend will exacerbate the force of hurricanes. Other scientists tell us this: the earthquake that violently interrupted the World Series was not the big one they are expecting for California. Nineteen hundred ninety-two set new records for number of tornados reported and for hurricane damage. Then came the Blizzard of '93!

Another concern is a recent scientific forecast that the earth is about due to be hit by a meteor of the magnitude of the one that, according to their postulations, so disrupted the earth's ecological systems that it caused the mighty dinosaurs to become extinct. If a meteorite did that to the dinosaurs . . . !

IMPACT ON FREEDOM

The conventional wisdom scenario unquestionably provides a better environment for the osmosis of freedom than any of the predictions by the contrarians. Indeed, the cause of freedom could be dealt a visceral blow by some of these events. In a worst-case scenario, the assignment to advance the present limits of freedom could be well termed "mission impossible." Yet, in this great nation, intrepid individuals have always risen to such a challenge.

Who are these contrarians? Perhaps their world view is similar to Aldous Huxley's, who wrote, "I was born wandering between two worlds, one dead and the other powerless to be born, and I have made in a curious way the worst of both." If so, we should give them scarcely a fleeting glance as we march forward in our gallant mission for the cause of liberty.

But with so many possibilities for something of major consequence to go wrong with the best-laid plans of mice and men, should we not seek a balance in the credence we give to these contrarians? Neither credulous nor unheeding may be that balanced position from which we can begin to draw useful, valid conclusions.

IMPACT ON BUSINESS

The vast majority of Americans do not like to hear these extremely negative views; we prefer science fiction novels or horror movies, not a prediction of the real thing. We fail to remember contrarians whose convictions made them rich: the Kennedy clan, for instance.

Most but not all changes have two sides. There are winners and losers. The common-wisdom folks are the losers when we find ourselves drawn into one of the contrarian's epochs. But interglobal thinkers have carefully listened to the doomsday messages, have counted the cost and thought through the ramifications. Interglobalists are sensitive to the early warning signals and, as often as not, they position themselves to take advantage of the change.

Chapter Nineteen

CONCLUSIONS

From the inward, outward and forward looks, the following Interglobal Age conclusions emerge.

One: Everyone everywhere wants to be free.

Two: Despots everywhere want to control as many people as they can.

Three: There is therefore constant conflict — even in nations now free.

Four: This intense struggle has given birth to the Interglobal Revolution.

Five: The Interglobal Revolution is being followed by the Interglobal Age.

Six: Dramatic changes, not all in the direction of the American model, can be expected.

Seven: Freedom is very costly: it emerges only when a strong leader arises with a critical mass of followers who prize liberty higher than life itself.

Eight: Freedom is difficult to maintain: those born free tend to be unwilling to pay the price for their children's freedom unless they are attacked in an overt act of war.

Nine: Life's greatest joys and fulfillments come from giving, not getting, and this unselfish spirit is at the core of the Interglobalist — one given to exporting freedom and free markets.

Ten: America must amend its selfishness if it is to succeed in the Interglobal Age.

Eleven: America's people and its media must be as dedicated to unselfish, idealistic Interglobalism as the counter-culturalists and the media were in the '60s if their "Me" syndrome is to be changed for the better.

Twelve: Interglobalism is the only secular cause that could rally enough citizens to effect this much-needed renewal of the soul of the United States.

Thirteen: The alternative is for America to follow Britain, Rome and Greece on the downward path reserved for has-beens.

Fourteen: There are formidable obstacles to accomplishing this American turnaround; the upward path is long and steep; the process is complex and the programs will have to be sound.

Fifteen: These integrated, coordinated programs include:
- Intensive interglobal business activities
- Political action
- Volunteerism
- Financial support for these three programs
- Enlistment of all nations in this great humanitarian endeavor.

Sixteen: Leaders must arise from all walks of life: business, the media, education, labor, industrial and professional associations, service clubs, churches, cultural groups, financial institutions, associations of youth and senior citizens and entertainers.

Seventeen: These leaders must take action NOW.

Eighteen: Henry Kaiser provided a role model for the interglobal businessman: an industrialist and a humanitarian who knew no geographic bounds.

Nineteen: Interglobal Age investments should be called "neo-capitalism."

Twenty: Successful entrepreneurs, managers, workers, investors, and the developers of new products and services must be venerated; the hedonistic anti-hero of the past three decades must be vanquished.

Twenty-one: The melting pot must be remelted: we must become one society, united in interglobal thought and action.

Twenty-two: Battles for global markets are replacing military battles; we are facing unprecedented worldwide economic competition.

Twenty-three: Old ways of doing business must yield to interglobalism in the face of this competition and the rapidity of political change.

Twenty-four: Profit opportunities abound for both large and small American businesses in the Interglobal Age — especially for those who are creative and patient!

PART FIVE

Fresh Strategies

Chapter Twenty

INTERNATIONAL OPERATIONS

The Interglobal Revolution has forever shattered old certainties and ways of doing business — even for the largest and most experienced multinational corporations.

POLITICAL CORPORATIONS

Battles for planetary markets will demand that our major corporations take a more active role in public affairs. The Chairman, Vice-Chairman, and Senior Chairman may spend much of their time with the world's political leaders. The battle between free-market forces and the protectionists may well be more important than the constant war with the competition.

These political leaders may become more sophisticated in their negotiations as they recognize the value of the markets. For instance, they may demand the construction of some manufacturing facilities in their own country, as the People's Republic of China does, complete with the provision of social welfare benefits for employees that in the West have been the responsibility of the individual or the government.

In his 1989 trip to Poland, President Bush bluntly told Solidarity that the private sector would bear the brunt of our foreign aid program to that destitute, emerging democracy. Business manifestly failed to perform the development function in post-colonial Africa. Do we have businessmen-statesmen? Will American shareholders, great pension-funds and insurance companies adapt to this interglobal reality?

Corporate management must continually sell the nations and the alliances of nations on the fact that it is in their long-term self-interest to trade freely with all nations. They also must be convinced that their own industries need to make the same pollution-control investments that ours are making.

Businessmen may labor alongside diplomats on such issues as terrorism and ethnic squabbles. American property and personnel in other countries must be respected and protected. Anti-American, even anti-anyone firefights, must be identified and quenched before they begin.

All this means that new business skills must be developed and new job descriptions written. Our people must learn new languages and become transcultural. Overseas posts must become important career pathways.

Products must be produced for as many cultures as possible, with quality control firmly in the hand of key corporate management, yet marketing decisions will probably be made by nationals, and product lines must be lengthened to serve as many market niches as possible.

Coca-Cola has been our most successful company in penetrating world markets. Local manufacturing of a standard product with marketing oriented toward the host culture works well for PepsiCo, too! Some large American enterprises need considerable fine-tuning on one or both of these fundamentals. Many need to refine their product line to give it more universal appeal. Others need to target more market niches with an expanded array of products. All but a few need to tailor merchandizing to each niche targeted. For instance, a recent Coke® TV commercial in Japan showed well-dressed, vivacious Japanese teenagers enjoying their product. Rise to the challenge, manufacturers of consumer products!

Manufacturers of industrial and business equipment should also expand their international activities. We can learn much from central planners, such as the Chinese. They established priorities for allocating their scarce resources. Being an agrarian empire, land conservation and reclamation are very important to them. Agricultural equipment, in a decade-long slump here, has a good market in many nations. Unfortunately, the smaller, cheaper Asian machines are often more suited to the largest markets — few can afford our power steering, insulated cabs, air-conditioning, and stereo systems.

Construction of facilities for the production of anhydrous ammonia, urea, and ammonium sulfate fertilizers will continue to be an opportunity for a few firms in the United States. James Boillot, Chief Executive Officer of the National Fertilizer Solutions Associations, expects a modest 2.9 percent annual increase in world use of nitrogen fertilizers during the '90s. American participants should be engineering companies, general contractors, subcontractors, and vendors of a wide range of specialized vessels, piping, fittings, and controls. Some see of a new wave of field equipment being purchased to more accurately spread the fertilizer and place it where it will not so easily find its way into the groundwater. A few even dare to dream of U.S.-style solid and liquid bulk handling making inroads in replacing the traditional fertilizer bags.

Communications is very high on the Chinese list. Fiberoptic cables are appropriate for the hundreds of millions of businesses and households that would jump at the chance to have a telephone installed at the prices we take for granted. In the meantime, a smaller and more affluent market is awaiting the opportunity to own a cellular phone.

Transportation is a severe bottleneck in much of Africa and Asia. For instance, China has plenty of coal, but can't get this simple commodity to vital industries, much less to all potential consumers. Unfortunately, hard currency shortages will often restrict Americans to the sale of know-how and the machinery for factories to produce locomotives, rail cars and trucks, rather than the sale of the equipment itself.

Housing will boom in nations that are rapidly industrializing. This will put pressure on our planet's forest resources. Unfortunately, assembly-line home building is still in the future. A Colorado group, however, has high hopes for a high-tech adobe process that is excellent from the standpoints of cost-effectiveness, insulation, and natural resource conservation.

Although our banks are no longer the world's largest, our financial institutions should remain major competitors in financing development in the Interglobal Age.

American financial institutions have fallen far behind the Japanese and Europeans. They were lured by greed into high-interest, long-term "safe" loans to the developing nations in the 1970s. These loans did not require appreciable oversight and were good for public relations at the time. During the 1980s, this policy has resulted in massive write-offs for many of America's larger banks.

It is now time for our financial community to aggressively enter the global marketplace in a mature, responsible way, or slip into oblivion. An appropriate way to address this market could be to work with banks' present customers in a partnership effort of business development and exportation of freedom. Globalization of these financial institutions will require the hiring of foreign individuals with talent and the ability to go all the way to the top. It will also require senior management to expand its horizons

138

with hands-off banking in nations that are desperately in need of improving their human rights records.

Never mind, bankers, that our largest institutions are no longer the world's biggest. Let's just make ours interglobal — and the best!

Sophisticated investors in the Interglobal Age will be balancing their portfolios among some twenty world-class stock markets and our own multinational corporations. The interglobal investor, like the interglobal corporate manager, will be a long-term player, not a day trader; he will have a humanitarian interest in his projects and the role they play in enhancing the lives of millions — many of whom are just beginning to emerge from abject poverty or subsistence. He will also be interested in the environmental impact of his investments. In fact, he may seek out environmental technologies for his portfolio. And, like the classical capitalists of yore, he will reserve about five percent of his funds for worthwhile start-ups — true venture capital injections into new interglobal businesses.

Service enterprises hold great promise. In China, the tourist hotels led the way in development as that nation opened herself to the West in the '80s. This script should be rerun in Eastern Europe and the C.I.S. in the '90s. These same countries need distribution networks to be created by private companies. Analysts believe there are profits to be made in replacing the unbelievably complex and cumbersome communist make-work systems with modern trucks and warehouses. Additionally, the citizens could be much better nourished if they could feast on food that has not been spoiled, spilled, or pilfered. Control of the latter may require a return to the shotgun-rider concept of our early stagecoach years.

American design/engineering/construction people should be quite aggressive in the world service sector, as should our consulting, accounting, and legal folks.

INTERGLOBAL STRATEGY

Henry Kaiser ranks among the all-time greats in American entrepreneurship and humanitarianism. The two were inseparable to this great man. His genius as an industrialist made him a legend in his own time. During World War II, a cartoon showed Mr. Kaiser, a fur-coated lady with a champagne bottle, and an admiral on a platform well above the hull of a ship, with welders still working on its construction. In the caption, Mr. Kaiser said, "Just start swinging lady, the ship will be there!"

Following World War II, Kaiser's fertile mind and well-heeled bank account set out to develop a number of international business enterprises. In fact, Mr. Kaiser was often informally referred to as a quasi-secretary-of-state, since he spent a great deal of his time flying around the globe working on business projects with government, industry, and financial leaders in many nations. He had a well-deserved reputation for his benevolent treatment of his employees, even providing hospitals where local service was inadequate. This unique blend of business and engineering know-how united with a humanitarian spirit drove him to take risks, and to appear to stretch himself, Kaiser Industries, and its satellite corporations well beyond each of their individual capabilities. For instance, an aluminum project in Ghana by his Kaiser Aluminum and Chemicals Corporation in the 1960s was called "highly speculative" by his peers. Subsequent political events in Africa, however, proved the critics wrong. This is not to say that Kaiser was without his failures — he failed to penetrate the automobile market after World War II with his "Henry J."

But this early interglobal thinker had a method to his seeming madness; he spread the political risks across as many countries as possible and spread the business risk across as many industries as possible. This strategy proved much more successful during his active business life than during the subsequent years when hired managers, who were only a small measure of the caliber of man Kaiser was, and who had little appreciation for his advanced philosophies, were guiding the company. These precepts are worth consideration at this juncture.

NUMBER ONE:
DEVELOP A GLOBAL STRATEGY

Do not be guided by projects that someone sells to you, nor by current events. In his case, his guideline was spreading the risk both politically and business-wise. Yet overriding this was his desire to establish productive private sector businesses that would benefit the people of this already shrinking globe.

NUMBER TWO:
CHOOSE YOUR PROJECTS CAREFULLY

Henry Kaiser spared almost no expense in developing a project. For instance, in the mid-1960s, when the specter of famine hung heavily over the Indian sub-continent and to a lesser degree over the rest of the world, Mr. Kaiser spent eighty million dollars to purchase a regional nitrogen fertilizer manufacturing company in the United States. His principal objective was to gain expertise in that fast-growing industry in order to build a nitrogen fertilizer plant in India with his partner, G.D. Birla. Later, he planned to parlay this experience into additional projects in nations such as Pakistan and Indonesia. Not content that he had done enough, Kaiser then beefed-up the management with the best international fertilizer and market analysts he could find. The study team was promptly launched to Asia, where two full-blown feasibility studies, including negotiations with governments, consumed a great deal of management time and were quite expensive. In the end, Kaiser implemented neither project. The government of India placed a new tax upon the Hindustani aluminum works (the joint venture between Kaiser and Birla), which dried up their cash flow — cash flow that was planned as equity capital for this fifty million dollar new project. The Pakistani project ultimately failed to go forward because of a reported lack of trust in potential joint venture partners.

The message is clear: even Henry Kaiser chose his targets carefully, analyzed them thoroughly, and proceeded with caution.

NUMBER THREE:
ASSUME AFFORDABLE DEBTS

Kaiser was highly experienced in utilizing all the available guarantees, and in financing from the United States government and host governments. He also often protected himself by having a strong, well-proven local partner. Yet he knew that some projects would fail. For Mr. Kaiser, an affordable risk was in the fifty-million-dollar to one-hundred-million dollar total project capital category, in an era when the dollar was worth three times its value in the 1990s. Decide what you can afford to lose.

NUMBER FOUR:
REINVEST PRUDENTLY

Kaiser always made provision for the repatriation of profits. But, unlike many Americans, he was willing, as in the case of the Indian aluminum venture, to reinvest a substantial portion of his cash flow in the country where the money was earned. Returning the principal sum to the United States from a nation that had good opportunities for expansion was not necessarily a criterion of his.

NUMBER FIVE: BE PATIENT

Even when in his eighties and with failing health, Kaiser was a patient investor. Like most business of the time, the feasibility studies were made with a discounted cash flow and alternative projects were compared for return on investment. However, the grand old man knew there were often problems in getting spare parts in some nations, and that labor productivity might not be what was expected. Therefore, some of the more elegant cash flow projections were heavily discounted by experienced international management.

Kaiser's patience also included patience with his local partner and the host governments. Some of his finest projects were turned down by competing industrialists from this country simply because the competitors lacked the patience to follow through with details they did not have to put up with in doing business here. Kaiser, the humanitarian, endured many of these procrastinations, yet had an interglobal sense about him that told him when further negotiations and exploration with a partner or a government would be unproductive.

NUMBER SIX: KEEP MOVING FORWARD

Executives under Henry Kaiser differed in their opinions as to whether the legendary man was a leader or a driver. This distinction may be immaterial, since his people were constantly on the move around the world looking for projects within certain well-specified boundaries, analyzing these potential ventures, and implementing them.

Kaiser was at his prime at a strategic juncture in history; he would often be one of the first important businessmen to arrive in a newly independent nation. But he was not on an ego trip nor was he a tourist. He was simply well aware of the benefits of being an early participant in an emerging economy: there were a limited number of viable projects of the scale desired by Kaiser, there were only a limited number of potential local partners in these immature, usually small economies, and early projects have the opportunity to hire the best workers, managers, and marketers.

INTERGLOBAL MANAGEMENT

All phases of management must be redefined in order to compete in the interglobal age: personnel, technologies, product lines, and markets. Most importantly, we must learn to further delegate and decentralize.

PERSONNEL

Everyone in an interglobal company must learn to think inter-globally. We source materials and products worldwide; we must now begin to hire the world's best people, wherever they are from and whatever language they speak. This is imperative because of competition and the delegation and decentralization that will be taking place.

America's best people must realize this: they must develop language skills, transcultural skills, and be willing to live abroad if they are not to be left behind. We have come full cycle from the 1950s, when upward mobility meant several moves: a field office, a regional center, and finally the home office. In the laid-back '80s, a young person chose the city where he wished to live, and then job-hopped. Substantial foreign experience will be demanded of tomorrow's top executives. So will flexibility and adaptability.

GLOBAL MARKETS

National Boundaries are becoming less and less important — mere wickets to be negotiated along the croquet course — some stickier than others, of course. We must manufacture to meet the world's standards, even if these specifications have been established by the Europeans or the Japanese.

Product lines will be determined by income levels, not by national boundaries. Therefore, management should give serious consideration to a system in which each product manager covers the globe. It will probably be necessary to have a different marketing strategy for different products in the line. National merchandisers can then tailor the message to the culture.

Market share, not short-term profits, must dominate our thinking. This is true because ultimately, market share will almost always produce cash flow. We must take the offensive and compete strongly throughout the world; America's largest companies cannot afford to lose by default in a market as large as Europe, Japan, or the Middle East.

Yes, Japan. Chief Trade Negotiator Carla A. Hills has established as her highest priority the fair treatment of our companies in that powerful commercial empire.

RESEARCH AND DEVELOPMENT

Product life spans are becoming shorter and shorter. No more resting on the laurels of successful commercialization of a new product. Efforts must be redoubled to make our own new widget obsolete — before the competition does.

Cheap labor is abundantly available to everyone. So are computers and the information they provide. Skilled, experienced personnel readily change companies these days. This leaves R&D with more of the burden of providing the long-term comparative edge.

It is time to establish research centers in Eastern Europe and the Commonwealth of Independent States, or bring the best individuals to our laboratories here. We must continually comb the world for existing breakthroughs. Such efforts could prove highly cost-effective.

Indeed, the gap between research by individuals or small, innovative firms and commercial adoption of a new technology may be the most profitable fishing hole for America's interglobal companies. But it takes a unique individual or team to sift through all of the chaff quickly and emerge with real gems — the products and services of tomorrow.

ALLIANCES

Sometimes the best people can't be hired; sometimes the best company in a given industry can't be acquired; sometimes the best technology can't be licensed. Joint ventures or other types of alliances often are the key to profits in a given nation or with a certain product line — and usually quicker and cheaper than classical growth from within.

Parker Drilling Company, for instance, invented the Heli-Rig and became the world's leader in land-rig technology. Parker now owns 24 of these oil drilling rigs, which can be transported to virtually any spot on the globe by a helicopter. They are already reported to have generated more than $1 billion in contract drilling revenues for the Tulsa firm, almost all of which was in foreign jungles and forests.

Chapter Twenty-One

NEOPHYTES

I f the multinational corporations must make drastic adjustments to compete — let alone prosper — how much more of a trauma is the dawning of the Interglobal Age for American businesses not presently significantly involved outside this country? Can neophytes penetrate the jungle and reach the village marketplace?

Staying in one's comfort zone is very important in a corporate culture. But with the future of America at stake, it is time for us to cast comfort aside and ask some basic questions.

THE ENTRANCE EXAM

Ancient Greek philosophers believed that the unexamined life is not worth living. Does it not then follow that in America — indeed, in all of the global village — the unexamined corporation is not worth investing in and working for — unexamined from the interglobal perspective? Yes, it is time for each of us to examine both ourselves and the enterprise into which we pour our funds, our prime time, and our talents.

In the "me-now" '80s, everything was self-centered and short-term. And why should individuals and endeavors reverse their field and suddenly convert to interglobal thinking? Won't it be a future generation that pays our fiddler in a muddled-down or melted-down America? No, says the present rate of change; time is fast running out.

Another question: in the Interglobal Age, a more ethical, more long-term-oriented age, what is the corporate responsibility to the community, to America, and to the entire village? President Bush in the 1990 State of the Union address told of recently holding his new grandbaby, and he said it put the affairs of state in perspective. Perhaps our board meetings and executive meetings should be attended by our children and grandchildren, or maybe we should pull the pictures out of our wallets and spend a minute with them before each issue is debated. How will each decision affect those to whom we will leave our worldly goods?

In the past, world events have had little more than curiosity value to most American businessmen. Are we, like Cain, finally being called into account as our brother's keeper? Or as his brother? Or is it just that we suddenly have five and a half billion neighbors?

Have you and your company seriously searched to see if you have a product, a service, a technology, a skill, or even an idea that would make life better for a reasonable number of people beyond our borders? If so, and if you found nothing conclusive, was a creative international consulting firm able to find a project for you? Do you have the resources to gain access to the business sector of the global village? If you could honestly answer "no" to all of the questions in this paragraph, smugness is not in order; please refer to the following chapter, "We the People."

Now, consider this question: if every business responds to the global challenge the way ours does, what will the United States be like for my children and grandchildren? True, not every organization needs a strong interglobal focus for this land to recover its leadership role, but the inertia is immense.

If not you and your company, who?
If not now, when?

YOUR STRATEGIC ANALYSIS

Interglobal Tenderfoot is the badge given to those with passing marks on the entrance examination. The tenderfoot always needs training and experience. Both cost money and take time.

A seminar on doing business in the Interglobal Age may be appropriate as the first step for some. Equally valid is this approach: proceed directly to a strategic analysis and preliminary corporate plan for interglobal action.

The format used in this book can be used as a starting point: the inward look at your interglobal strengths and weaknesses; the outward look at your worldwide industry; the forward look, with as many points of view as you deem to be of value; your strategic options; your corporate interglobal strategy in twenty words or less; the steps for implementing this strategy; the approximate capital cost and timing of each step; and a likely financing plan.

Involve as wide a spectrum of knowledgeable people in this procedure as possible. Experienced outsiders can be especially helpful. Since it is a preliminary exercise, it is normally wise not to overkill with either time or money. An infantry officer would call it a "preliminary estimate of the situation." Although the company five years from now likely will look far different from this early document, do not despise the discipline. It forces you to think through the fundamentals of interglobalism as they relate to your situation.

Two of the decisions not explicitly set forth in this outline are the products or services to be taken to the village marketplace and the people in the village you will be dealing with.

There are two philosophies in approaching the strategic analysis and preliminary interglobal business plan: the think-tank approach and the formal approach. Since most management teams have some feel for their industry around the world and also know people who have in-depth knowledge, and since the imprecise nature of this first iteration is recognized by all concerned, many will opt for a few skull sessions augmented by phone calls and easily obtainable information (in-house, trade association, or trade publication).

Purists, however, will want a more exhaustive and formal study. So will those worried about the political impact of a less-than-professional paper floating around the company over their signature. Additional data can be collected from state trade promotion agencies and the U.S. Department of Commerce regional field office. Some will regard as within their scope a trip to Washington to visit with Commerce Department specialists and the commercial counselors in embassies and trade missions.

THE PRELIMINARY FEASIBILITY STUDY

Assuming a favorable management response to the strategic analysis and plan, the next step is a preliminary feasibility study of the first project or the first phase of the plan. Foreign travel is necessary, as is an able consultant for the rank tenderfoot. Even the seasoned tourist will lack the perception needed for accurate field evaluation; a wide gulf exists between the tourist and the interglobalist.

If the think-tank approach was used in the strategic analysis, it will be wise to gather the information suggested for the formal study before proceeding abroad. With this information, the foreign work can be planned.

The first stop in the targeted foreign capital should be the commercial section of the American Embassy, which often is not located in the embassy, whose main function is political. The commercial-section usually has lists of people you will want to see. More importantly, they normally can convey important updates and nuances that are not in their written reports.

If your team is larger than two people, you will then probably divide the work into various responsibilities: government and legal, market and marketing, manufacturing, financial, and cultural are typical assignments for a full team studying a project of some scale. The preliminary team usually limits itself to about two weeks in one nation. Neophytes will want to guard against making early decisions based on common wisdom in the United States; it takes some time and empathy to research foreign projects. One reason for making this trip is to collect primary data and talk personally with the individuals with whom your company will be doing business or from whom you will be seeking to take a market share.

The final preliminary feasibility study task is reaching a team consensus, report writing, and presentations. If the findings are favorable, management should be asked — no, challenged — to proceed with the next step: a detailed business plan from which project financing can be obtained.

THE BUSINESS PLAN

The plot thickens. Your accounting, consulting, and legal firms become involved. Fact-finding and negotiating trips may be needed. Patience now becomes an important factor as each "i" is dotted and each "t" is crossed. You are really learning to be an interglobalist as your culture clashes with the culture of foreign bureaucrats and private businessmen; you learn to flex; you learn to touch bases you never knew existed.

The business plan, however, can be completed before all the host governmental approvals are obtained — providing you believe such approval will not be denied. Since excellent books are available on the preparation of the business plan and many practitioners are expert in this field, a discussion of this advanced and complicated step is considered beyond the scope of this book.

FINANCING

The international financial community should provide the necessary financing for a stable company with a thorough business plan. Again, those delicate negotiations and contracts are outside the scope of this introductory volume. Able help is available and should be used.

Interglobal financing, however, goes beyond creative financing —at a time when banks in the United States are properly returning to the conservative cloth from which they were cut.

Expanding the search for financing to overseas institutions is not interglobal financing; there is nothing new there. But a prominent hotel chain has provided a model for interglobal financing. At the first sign that the market could support a fine new facility, and long before the competition would give it a serious thought, the high-profile chairman would jet into the target city with wonderful news: "We are planning a world-class hotel!" Amid much fanfare, he and his cohorts would perform all of the due procedures, complete a feasibility study and artist's rendition, and emerge with a management contract and virtually one hundred percent local financing. Observers were astounded at his ability to get money in some awfully poor nations.

Almost without exception these unlikely ventures prospered, and the investors were also delighted with the prestige the hotel gave their growing community.

Most American companies, not now involved offshore, see financing the additional component to their business as a big obstacle to going interglobal. Other, more perceptive groups see the leveraged opportunities abroad as a prime reason for international expansion.

Two of the best-known sources of funding are in Scotland and Singapore. The Scottish Development Agency has helped several American companies with low-cost loans and grants for worker training. Singapore, a financial center for bustling Southeast Asia, offers one of the best packages — the promotional book weighs a pound! The package includes capital for equipment purchases, low-interest loans, and a tax holiday for up to ten years.

Another plus: foreign investors and banks may have a greater appreciation for new technology than domestic banks and venture capital companies.

IMPLEMENTATION

It is now time to execute the agreements and obtain final approvals from all necessary governmental agencies. The elapsed time and the money spent will vary widely. In a centrally planned economy, the time may be two years, and hundreds of thousands of dollars may have been spent. China, for instance, has been requiring about twenty chops (British and Hong Kong lingo for official government seals) and about a year. In the most open nations, little more time may be required than for a similar project here, but travel and communication will definitely cause more money to be expended. Contingencies for delays and cost overruns should be allocated in planning.

FREEDOM SPIN-OFF

Your personnel can be doing some language and cultural studies here at home while the preceding steps are unfolding. These skills will be invaluable in the business and can also be used at close range to discreetly promote the liberties and freedoms we enjoy. Management may be surprised to see how many bright Americans will be eager to work for them overseas — many of our younger citizens are already beginning to think interglobally!

A COMMONWEALTH OF INDEPENDENT STATES OPPORTUNITY

For some businessmen, the appropriate programs for exporting freedom can be directly related to their own company operations and are potentially quite profitable. This is true for those engaged in the basics of food and agriculture. Monsanto Company, a major pesticide producer, was one of the first American firms to establish a marketing outpost in Moscow when Mikhail Gorbachev began opening his vast market.

Agriculture is one field where America still holds a commanding lead over the rest of the world. Americans involved in this giant industry of food production, processing, transportation, marketing, and input supply range from giant Monsanto-sized corporations down to individual farmers tilling a couple of sections of land. Since much of the industry is seasonal, many could spend a summer or winter engaging in technology transfer, education in the entrepreneurial skills, teaching basic work ethics, promoting American values, and developing a new business enterprise.

One American agribusiness firm sees an opening to export freedom while making a profit in the new Commonwealth of Independent States. This small organization contemplates establishing a network comprising at least the following technologies and skills:

Consulting and Work Services

As with the green revolution twenty years ago, the heart of any agricultural program is a technological package that can be understood by the farmer and that results in sizable increases in both yields and profits. To convey this technology transfer infor-

150

mation to rice farmers in Southeast Asia, who farm only a few acres with the help of an oxen or two, the county agent approach was used. In the C.I.S., information must be communicated to farm managers who are well trained in the science and art of farming and who have access to the latest information in their nation. Industrial sales techniques could be more appropriate there. Nevertheless, there are some major holes in the C.I.S. information and management systems. For instance, the American consortium contemplates placing portable soil testing laboratories in a van and doing on-site evaluations staffed by a technical person who can make immediate recommendations to the farm chairman. Why go to this bother? One of their group visited with a Soviet laboratory manager at an international soil testing symposium and found that the lazy farmers, who have lacked incentives, were forced to send in samples of their soil each year, but put the laboratory results in the drawer and did what they had been accustomed to doing. When the crops are growing, television cameras equipped with infrared lenses and backed by tissue testing procedures can determine how well the crop is growing while there is yet time to make adjustments by such procedures as foliar nutrient applications, additional irrigation water, or the application of a plant growth regulator.

IRRIGATION SYSTEMS

The potential for increasing farm productivity through groundwater irrigation in the Commonwealth of Independent States is considerable, since most irrigation both there and in China uses only surface water from streams and lakes. Therefore, the group contemplates the establishment of a manufacturing plant in the Soviet Union to build portable water well drilling rigs mounted on a large truck. An American manufacturer of such rigs, who also has an international division that is very active in the Middle East and Latin America, is standing ready to proceed with this component of the overall project. The chief executive of this division, who was an early interglobalist, expects that it will be necessary to place a quality control person in the field to provide quality assurance for both major equipment suppliers and the assembly plant. This hard-nosed individual will not allow materials to be shipped if specifications are not met or exceeded — a revolutionary concept for the lackadaisical former workers' paradise.

This group is also recruiting an American manufacturer of center pivot irrigation systems. Such systems now can be computer controlled for optimal moisture application and conservation.

Soil Amendments

A major problem in the arid and semi-arid regions of the former Soviet Union confronts the group that plans to use state-of-the-art American technologies to do contract reclamation work. The group plans first to export from this country, then to produce in the C.I.S., an extensive product line of plant growth regulators. Some of these sophisticated products are applied to the soil, some are used as seed treatments, some are used in conjunction with fertilizers that are applied near the seed to enhance early plant growth, some are mixed with contact herbicides to reduce crop damage, and some are sprayed on the plant at certain stages of growth. All have a common objective: to increase yields.

Genetic Technologies

Although the number of plant scientists engaged in plant breeding in the C.I.S. may now outnumber those in the United States, their technology lags far behind that of even the small, specialized breeders and seed companies in the United States. For instance, one breadgrain breeding organization produces grain that can increase the protein level of bread to the point that minimal supplemental protein is required — a boon where meat is in short supply and quite expensive. Coincidentally, these varieties yield as well or better than the best Russian wheats. Another small American seed company has developed commercial hybrid sunflowers, which in tests in India, side-by-side with the leading C.I.S. sunflower varieties, has produced yields two to three times higher than the Russian competition. It may be necessary for the soil to be treated with a common pesticide at the time of planting in order to keep these American varieties from being attacked by a soil-borne disease common to Europe. Commercial restraint strains, however, are expected by the U.S. plant breeders within one to two years.

Another oil seed, rapeseed, is being developed by several American institutions. These new varieties have a commanding advantage over most of the commercial rapeseed planted in the Commonwealth of Independent States.

Agri-Industrial Technologies

Reinvestment is not expected to be limited to inputs for the grains and the oil seeds. Therefore, the American organization expects to develop a combination animal feed and pulp industry in the north of Russia where the world's greatest reservoir of timber suitable for pulp is available to baseload the animal feed industry with a high-energy feed to replace imported corn. The pulp and paper products can be sold in Europe for hard currency. This Cellumaster process has been proven with five commercial plants in the United States, and is essentially a new pulping technology that utilizes the hemicellulose and lignin waste to produce animal feeds and composite plastics.

GRAND STRATEGY

When confronted with the possibility that the Soviets will resort to neo-communism, and perhaps even launch a new round of expansionism unmatched in their history, leaders of the American group responded that they have indeed counted the cost. But they believe a cogent approach to transition from the unworkable commune farming system to their strategic plan, working within the system, could provide the Kremlin leadership with a rational plan whereby they could make the change from their present bankrupt society, to one that is market oriented. Furthermore, the Americans say, once these gains are seen by the world, repressive Communist regimes could be encouraged to follow suit — even though in many cases, major changes may await the death of existing warlords.

Then again, we may not need to wait long; remember, the Chinese are ever pragmatic.

START-UPS

We have seen opportunities for large and small companies. The interglobal challenge should also give birth to American start-ups. Such new ventures have a distinct advantage: the organization can be one hundred percent interglobal in every way . . . no need for old dogs to learn new tricks.

Simply start with an idea or a technology, pull a management team together (Richard M. White, Jr., in *The Entrepreneurs Manual*, provides one model), raise seed capital for the preliminary feasibility study and the business plan, and you are well on your way.

THE BLIND POOL

Unfortunately, many would-be entrepreneurs don't really have a great new idea or technology. A solution to this problem is to retain an interglobal consultant for a couple of days of brainstorming. This solution also works if you have the concept in focus but don't know the territory.

153

A bolder, yet almost sure-fire strategy, is to tour the former Soviet bloc in search of both market niches and technologies. Although our nation has a problem in this area, the East easily wins the prize for failing to bring its research projects to the marketplace. These nations have their full share of Ph.D.-level scientists, engineers, and agriculturalists . . . and their salaries are very low.

Simply network your way through the markets and technologies in your chosen industry until you find the fit you want. Bureaucracies are wonderful fishing holes for the nimble-minded. A certain petroleum broker loves to regale his peers with his exploit in purchasing a product from one department of a major oil company, taking the elevator to another floor and reselling it to another department's buyer.

Perhaps you can find use for a factory and work-force that formerly produced weapons. Or, you may want to hire a world-class scientist to develop a family of products.

THE ULTIMATE ADVANTAGE

In the final analysis, it may be bravery in commercial combat and stubborn refusal to quit that will be the most distinguishing marks of the interglobalist. After all, warlords must be defeated on their own turf — without stooping to their below-the-belt jabs and kicks.

It was just such an indomitable spirit as this that launched America and made her great. The slender, grand old man in the tall hat is still looking for citizens who, like Admiral David G. Farragut, will leave the safe, sheltered home ports, and, when the chips are down, will shout, "Damn the torpedoes. Full speed ahead!"

Twenty-Two

WE THE PEOPLE

I t is not enough for our companies presently engaged in international business to redouble their efforts; it is not even enough that we double or triple the number of our businesses engaged in international commerce. If the United States is to emerge as a leader in the interglobal village, all our citizens must unite behind the effort of these interglobal entrepreneurs . . . just as the Japanese people helped their nation excel in the pre-interglobal era.

Exporting freedom is a new enterprise to most Americans and their institutions. Therefore, considerable study and expert help will be needed in order to develop appropriate programs.

POLITICAL ACTION

Every candidate for national political office would quickly affirm his concurrence with the need for America to prudently pursue a course that encourages human rights, freedom, and democracy throughout the world. Indeed, our government has been too long at the forefront of exporting freedom. Analysts who study the failure of the new republics in Africa to achieve their desired results point out that our government often was instrumental in getting the appropriate form of government in place at the time of the demise of the colonialists, but our private sector failed to follow through with investments, business ventures, and volunteer programs on a sufficient scale to prevent some of them from falling prey to Communism, tribalism, and old-fashioned graft.

Therefore, concerned Republicans and Democrats alike should continually make known to candidates and current office holders the high priority they place on the export of freedom. It is not a partisan issue!

VOLUNTEERISM

Jimmy Carter may be the best ex-president the United States has had since Herbert Hoover. Certainly, Carter's efforts to provide housing through his personal carpentry work; to feed the hungry; and to bring peace and freedom to the peoples of the world, provide an outstanding model for volunteerism. Carter travels the globe in a private jet, is a guest in presidential mansions, and uses his influence to promote the altruistic causes that initially lured him from obscurity in Plains, Georgia. In Ethiopia, Carter attempted to negotiate an accord between the Marxist government in Addis Abbaba and the freedom fighters. In the "feed-the-hungry" arena, he is ably assisted by agronomist Norman Borlaug, a 1970 Nobel Peace Prize winner.

Not all Americans have the resources available to Carter, whose foundation's funding comes largely from abroad, but all can emulate his dedication and zeal. For some American volunteers, liaison with foreign students at a local college or university will be the best opportunity to promote the cause of freedom. The future leader of a foreign nation, or one of its influential leaders, may be today's lonely student who welcomes a family's offering to be "his other home away from home."

Campus organizations, including the social fraternities and sororities, could become much more active in cultivating the foreign students who are so often unnoticed among them. Upon returning to their native lands, these strangers should not have to remember that other foreign students were their only support system while in America.

FINANCIAL AND MORAL SUPPORT

Some older American citizens may feel more comfortable in simply supplying financial and moral support to organizations and individuals involved in exporting freedom. One possibility is for grandparents to provide all or part of the financial aid to a young person working overseas as a short-term volunteer. Mature Americans without such financial means can always adopt pen pals, collect and send suitable reading material, and encourage younger people to become involved in the freedom-exporting campaign.

ENLISTING THE FREE WORLD

Although the previously cited polls show that Americans are twice as prone to volunteerism and outreach with freedom as are their European and Japanese counterparts, Americans, both in government and the private sector, should make their major goal the enlistment in the freedom crusade of governments, businesses, and volunteer organizations in every free-world country. One American institution or sector cannot win that battle alone. Neither can America alone. We must find ways to spark the interest of every person, organization, and nation that claims to uphold freedom!

LIFESTYLE

So much for the actions, movements, and programs. Our attention must now turn to the organizations, which, in concert with our interglobal businesses, will complete the task of spreading our economic and political systems throughout our planetary community.

But first, before the organizations, individuals must change. We must become more responsible to society; we must become more industrious — pursuing excellence in all areas of life; we must delight in saving, not spending; we must learn to use another language; we must learn about our world and its people groups; we must begin thinking globally; we must unite with others for the long-term betterment of all mankind. Unless these things happen deep in our hearts, unless we are delivered from our addictions, unless we turn from violence, lust, and rape, unless white-collar crime and shirking are forsaken, unless we curb conspicuous consumerism, unless we cease to be single-issue voters demanding more and more for ourselves while contributing less and less; unless we still our grumbling and complaining — we will go the way of the Babylonian and Persian civilizations.

FAMILY

Television — with its anti-family bias, its sex outside the bounds of marriage, and its macabre violence — has replaced family life. Parents have abandoned their children to an electronic marvel that teaches them the demonic and deliberately drives a wedge between the father and his children. How wise!

Yes, the love, acceptance, discipline, and the teaching of moral and religious values must also be restored to the home if we are to avoid sinking deeper in our decaying swamp of irresponsibility. Parents must teach in the same manner as the television set: by example. Husbands must show love, concern and courtesy to their wives — and wives to their husbands; everyone must spend quality time truly listening to the current concerns of each family member; parents must display positive attitudes toward their schools, teachers, police, and other public officials, and concern must be shown for the needs of others throughout the global community.

But that's not all. Interglobal thinking must be instilled at a very early age; pre-school may be the best age to begin learning a second language. European families practice on each other during leisurely family meals — some setting three or four meals a week aside, with the language of a different neighboring nation spoken at each meal. It's never too early to begin talking of exciting career possibilities around the world. And wise parents begin talking about schooling that will prepare for such useful work long before their peers begin talking about their favorite schools and major subjects.

Interglobalism begins at home. But it only begins there; interglobalists must work through many of our institutions.

YOUTH ORGANIZATIONS

Interglobal parents, school administrators, and bright young people should organize international clubs in the secondary schools.

The squeaky-clean 4-H clubs have long provided an excellent model for international youth exchanges. City youth groups will do well to follow their excellent leadership. International career guidance should receive strong emphasis in our high schools.

COLLEGES AND UNIVERSITIES

Student exchange programs can play a vital role. Grand Canyon University of Phoenix, Arizona, was one of the first to reach out to the Soviet Union. They, in 1989, concluded a student exchange pact with the Kazakhstan Ministry of Education, and began with thirteen Americans flying to the Kazakhstan Soviet Socialist Republic. These exchanges are important because they let others see the best of America, and they are especially important for future leaders; they also can open avenues for other contracts such as in the area of business.

CHURCHES

The small, rural-oriented Mennonite denominations have been pacemakers in international volunteerism. These thrifty, hardworking Americans, during the years since World War II, have developed many farming and household techniques and products that can very easily be used with the limited resources typical of the non-developing nations. Their volunteerism, in addition to its timeliness at the lowest level of the economy, has also been popular because of their restraint in proselytizing. The Mennonites believe that Jesus Christ should be seen through their lives, not their words. All of their young people are encouraged to spend two years in volunteer work — a noble objective for all!

Descriptive linguist Bruce Olsen has been remarkably successful in exporting freedom in Colombia. Living with a primitive tribe, he did not attempt to impose Western culture on them, but taught them the precepts of Christianity in ways they could understand in their cashless, communal society. Cooperatives were formed for marketing farm products, with profits accruing to schools and medical clinics. When Olsen was taken prisoner by Communist rebels, because of the effectiveness of his independent ministry, some fifty tribal groups met and petitioned his release. Meanwhile, Olsen was teaching his illiterate guards how to read and write. Investigation was made by the rebel band in the field and it was ascertained that Olsen, although a gringo, had indeed been working for the good of the poorest people in the nation. This local group concluded it was in the best interest of the Communist insurgency to release Olsen. The national Communist hierarchy, however, mandated his death at the hands of a firing squad; a benevolent *Norteamericano* did not fit their dogma. When the shots rang out, Olsen did not fall. Captors who had been touched by his compassion had placed blank bullets in the executioners' rifles. Freedom exporter Olsen was then freed after nine months in captivity. After taking a brief rest, he is now taking his program to fifteen new tribes.

CULTURAL GROUPS

The Polish-American Congress may be the largest and best-organized cultural group in the United States; it certainly has had an excellent opportunity to strike a telling blow for freedom! Under the able direction of Ed Moskal, this Chicago-based organization represents one hundred Polish-related organizations and provides an umbrella for approximately thirteen hundred local Polish-American groups. In the past, they have funneled large quantities of money and material into Poland and are now actively seeking to help businessmen develop a private sector in that important nation. Their example should inspire other cultural organizations to strengthen themselves, take whatever action is possible at this time, and prepare for future openings.

ENTERTAINERS

Because the U.S. is the entertainment center of the world, many foreigners are eager to attend concerts, lectures, and American theater productions on tour. Impact Productions in 1989 hired a Soviet promotion firm to provide bookings in several cities. The results were mixed: in some cities, the concerts by the American group had to be canceled. They played to standing-room-only audiences during the weekend they were in Kiev, the capital of the restless Ukraine. Tom Newman, star of the group, reports they are ready to go again; in spite of the cumbersome movement of production equipment, i.e., stage set-up and striking of massive sets complete with scenery, sound amplification equipment, strobe and set lighting, special-effect devices such as smoke machines, makeup supplies, props, and full-line costuming for a complete cast of men and women. The result of this effort is well worth the exhausting requirements surrounding tour production, Newman believes.

LABOR UNIONS

Trade unions can play a unique role in exporting freedom. Many of the former Soviet bloc nations have forgotten how to work, have forgotten the discipline involved in producing quality products. Communists have long attempted to use the International Labor Organization (I.L.O.), as a front organization; it is now time for American unionists, from the professionals to rank and file, to become involved in volunteerism, exhorting and demonstrating to their compatriots abroad the value of quality craftsmanship, honest work, and loyalty to one's employer and union. Solidarity has paved the way for such independent unions to be established in a Communist empire.

INDUSTRY ASSOCIATIONS

Most national industrial associations are in some way affiliated with an international association. American activism in these international groups could provide a springboard for exporting freedom to nations desiring to increase their knowledge of various industries.

PROFESSIONAL ORGANIZATIONS

The situation with professional organizations is very similar to that of the labor unions and the industrial associations. American professionals, in their contacts with foreigners, could emphasize the vital role the American system has had in their success and in their professional and personal fulfillment.

SERVICE CLUBS

Service clubs can take a lead in direct contacts as well as in the establishment of new clubs around the world and the promotion of wider programs for exporting freedom. Although these clubs were primarily formed to serve the communities in which they were located, the uplift provided by the idealism of the freedom export campaign will also benefit the organization sponsoring such an international outreach.

Some folks from Omaha, for instance, were quick to reestablish their international service club in Warsaw after Solidarity took charge there.

RETIREMENT ORGANIZATIONS

Imagine the positive impact that the American Association for Retired People (A.A.R.P.) could have in promoting volunteerism in the freedom effort, if it threw its considerable resources and influence behind this freedom program. Instead of just being tourists, many members could become involved in volunteer projects.

LOCAL GOVERNMENTS

The Sister City International program could be greatly expanded by some cities currently participating in the program, and hundreds of new American cities could be encouraged to liaison with similar cities in nations urgently in need of seeing firsthand what American human rights, private enterprise, and democracy are all about. It was launched in 1956, when President Dwight D. Eisenhower called for massive exchanges between Americans and the people of other lands. Hundreds of American cities responded and today are carrying out exchanges with cities in about ninety nations of the world. The ideal affiliation involves a large number of citizens and organizations in the paired communities engaged in continuing projects of mutual interest. Tucson, Arizona, for instance, is paired with Alma Alta in central Asia; both are located in a desert region. Business relations are not enough. Cultural exchanges also provide an excellent and enduring forum for the transfer of the tenets of freedom.

STATE GOVERNMENTS

Many states are getting involved in helping businesses within their borders become established as exporters. Some now have offices in Europe and Japan. Again, the infusion of a fresh freedom-exporting campaign would be highly beneficial to their existing programs and would involve people who would not otherwise be touched by their organizations.

THE FEDERAL GOVERNMENT

The United States government has been our first line of offense in upholding and promoting human rights and democracy! A multitude of agencies are involved, but the State Department assumes primary responsibility. Former President Bush was criticized both by his political foes and by the State Department career diplomats for appointing persons with a history of large political campaign donations as ambassadors. Most, however, were leading businessmen who have a wide circle of influential friends.

This perceived disadvantage could be converted to an advantage; these ambassadors could share their new excitement about international affairs with their friends here. Thus, a new echelon of freedom exporters could quickly be brought to the battle line as the Bush appointees are replaced by Clinton people. Further, most of them are businessmen; they now can join the interglobal neophytes club, returning to their former overseas post in a business context.

The Commerce Department has offices in trade centers all over the world. Each office is responsible for a geographic area in the country where it is located. Therefore, even if there is not a commercial consulate in a city or town where you wish to do business, there is an officer responsible for gathering data in that location.

Likewise, the Agriculture Department has offices in many of the same locations as the Department of Commerce. They usually share office facilities and work closely together. The scope of this department has been reduced, in recent years, to concentrating on assisting with the market development and marketing of American farm products.

The periodic reports filed by these two departments are available through their offices in the United States and are one of the most important sources of current information for international businesses. Each also maintains country or area specialists in Washington.

NEW ORGANIZATIONS

It is usually difficult to mobilize existing organizations to meet new challenges. Therefore, Interglobal Clubs should be organized around the world to stimulate business development and freedom. Interglobal idealists of the world, unite! If only we could generate a fraction of the momentum Marx developed with his cell groups. . . . Perhaps we should start young — with high school and university Interglobal clubs!

Chapter Twenty-Three

ASK NOT WHAT THE WORLD . . .

The charisma of President John F. Kennedy stirred the young at heart with the phrase, "Ask not what your country can do for you, but what you can do for your country." Yet the idealistic rhetoric even of a leader of such magnitude had little impact on the United States in the face of the great counter-cultural revolution of the '60s. JFK was brutally assassinated during his third year in office, and anti-idealism soon raged angrily across America.

President Kennedy, when shot in Dallas on November 22, 1963, was on his way to deliver a speech with this ending:

> We in this country, in this generation, are — by destiny rather than choice — the watchmen on the walls of world freedom. We ask, therefore, that we may be worthy of our power and responsibility, that we may exercise our strength with wisdom and restraint, and that we may achieve in our time and for all time the ancient vision of peace on earth, goodwill toward men. That must always be our goal . . . For as was written long ago, "Except the Lord keep the city, the watchman waketh but in vain."

By the late 1970s, the next Democratic president, Jimmy Carter, made a nationally televised speech in which he spoke of a "Crisis of confidence, striking at the very heart and soul and spirit of our national will." Carter had prepared for this speech by spending two weeks of private soul-searching.

"Too many of us now tend to worship self-indulgence and con-sumption . . . human identity is no longer defined by what one does, but, by what one owns." This attitude, he contended, had contributed to a paralysis of government in which special interests prevent action on the behalf of national interest.

Richard Darman, the Director of the Office of Management and Budget, in a 1989 speech to the National Press Club, concurred with Carter's analysis. He cited our preoccupation with "political Mau-Mauism" and the "mindless cannibalism" of recent bitter political fights. He also condemned cultural "now-nowism": a shorthand label for our collective short-sightedness; our obsession with the here and now; our reluctance to adequately address the future . . . in our public policy, and in our private behavior, consuming today as if there is no tomorrow. "The deficit is but one more system of our now-nowism," he added.

At this writing, that federal budget deficit stands above four trillion dollars!

So, America went steadily downhill as a result of a youth revolution that soon spread even to the citadels of national power under both political parties and various presidents. The '90s probably offer the United States its last chance to return to the values that made us great — and to greatness itself. A new generation of idealists must emerge. Not only have we changed, but an Interglobalist Revolution has taken place since the euphoric days of Kennedy's Camelot. A few intellectuals of his day were speaking of the emerging global village; it is now a political and business reality.

"What can I do for my country" is now too small a question to accomplish an American turnaround. The only question today that is large enough to rekindle the fires of idealism that burned so brightly on this continent for well over two centuries is this: "What can I do for my world?"

The idealist must believe that love is more powerful than hate. We proved that principle in World War II: our love of freedom was more powerful than the hate Hitler whipped up against the peoples he wished to conquer. We must again rise to that level of practical idealism. Love for the oppressed, the downtrodden, the hungry, the huddled masses who hope against all reason for freedom and for economic opportunity. In so doing, America can experience a revival of its selfish soul. A revival of compassion that can spread throughout the earth.

And we must also make it clear that the profit motivation, too, is honorable, when balanced with the ideals of freedom and justice.

The ideal of exporting freedom and private enterprise as America's great crusade of the 1990s and beyond is an old-fashioned battle. Individuals will influence individuals. Perhaps your involvement will not produce results as great as Jimmy Carter's or Bruce Olson's — although some may have a greater effect — but you *can* have an influence. An overseas sphere of influence, however small, when combined with that of hundreds of thousands of other Americans, can make a crucial difference.

And the business you save, indeed, the nation you save, may be your own.

165

PART SIX

Epilogue